Therapeutic Inspirations Volume I

CW00456808

Therapeutic Inspirations Volume I

Fiona Biddle

and

Shaun Brookhouse

with

Susan Martin

UK Academy of Therapeutic Arts and Sciences Ltd.

©UK Academy of Therapeutic Arts and Sciences, Fiona Biddle & Shaun Brookhouse 2008

Published by

UK Academy of Therapeutic Arts and Sciences Ltd
16 St Philips Rd, Burton on the Wolds, Loughborough, LE12 5TS
Tel: 01509 881811
Email: info@ukacademy.org
Internet: www.ukacademy.org

The right of Stuart Biddle and Fiona Biddle to be identified as authors of this work has been asserted by them in accordance with the Copyright, Designs and Patents Act 1988.

All rights reserved. No part of this publication may be reproduced, stored in a retrieval system, or transmitted in any form or by any means, electronic, mechanical, photocopying, recording or otherwise, without the prior permission of the publishers, or a licence permitting restricted copying in the United Kingdom issued by the Copyright Licensing Agency, 90 Tottenham Court Road, London W1P 0LP.

ISBN 0-9544604-4-8

Note
Neither the publishers nor the authors will be liable for any loss or damage of any nature occasioned to or suffered by any person acting or refraining from acting as a result of reliance on the material contained in this publication.

Printed in the UK by Lightning Source

CONTENTS

INTRODUCTION

Since August 2003, the UK Academy of Therapeutic Arts and Sciences has been publishing an Ezine, called Inspirations which has been sent out to anyone within the therapy community who has requested it. In each issue we have had a tip on practice building, research, motivation and therapy, and only then, right at the end of the ezine, do we have the "sales bit"!

When we reached our 100th edition, it was suggested that we should collate the information contained into a publication. Certainly we didn't want the ideas to disappear, and so we have undertaken this task with the help of Susan Martin, a colleague and good friend from Southampton.

Thanks to Susan for her excellent work in putting this book together!

Thanks also to all those who have agreed to have their contributions included in this book. We are very grateful to you all!

Finally, we would like to encourage any reader who has ideas about therapy to share them with us for inclusion in future editions. Simply email info@ukacademy.org

Thanks in advance, and we hope you enjoy, and benefit from reading this book!

PRACTICE BUILDING TIPS

Do you value who you are and what you do?

Many people in the therapeutic arena undervalue themselves and what they do. Many courses encourage the belief that therapy is a vocation and some even suggest that charging money (or what might be described as a reasonable amount of money) is a bad thing. For many, of course, this career is a vocation, but does that mean you don't deserve to be properly rewarded for what you do?

Therapy is VALUABLE! Very valuable. You are helping your clients to improve their lives (aren't you?) You are a valuable member of society.

How comfortable do you feel about these statements? If you feel any discomfort then we would encourage you to examine your beliefs and values.

If you do not value yourself or your therapy, your clients and potential clients will not either. This process of valuing is essential to running a successful practice. Presumably you want to be successful, for yourself, your clients, your family, your community..... In fact everyone will benefit from your success, even your competitors, because if you raise the profile of your therapy, and the perceived value, so it will help them!

It is ok to need money and to be paid appropriately for your services. The word "appropriate" is key. Too much belittles you and your therapy as much as too little. Be realistic and enjoy the process of valuing yourself and what you do!

What are you proud of?

When I (Fiona) first qualified as a hypnotherapist, I was not proud of my qualification. This, I now believe, affected my practice. I have since undertaken several more courses of which I am proud. I am proud of the work that I did, and what I achieved. This makes a huge difference to how I feel as I market myself as a therapist. I am proud of the therapy I offer and of my skills and knowledge. This, I am sure, comes over to clients and gives them confidence.

What are you proud of? How does or can this affect your marketing?

What are you not proud of? What can you do about this?

A final point: it is vital to differentiate pride from arrogance. Only you will know for yourself how you feel. Others may label your confidence and pride in yourself as arrogance (as has happened with me), and for some the idea of pride being a deadly sin will affect how they view your feelings. Others may find your pride a threat to them. How your deal with these things is your choice, but it all comes down, as usual, to awareness!

Newspaper advertising

Newspaper advertising seems to be something that is more successful in some areas than in others. For example when I (Fiona) lived in Exeter, which has one daily local evening paper, I found small lineage adverts to consistently bring in a good return. However when I moved to Loughborough, I found newspaper advertising to be a waste of time. Perhaps this is due to there being a much larger choice of papers which cover a much larger geographical area.

Our suggestion would be to try it out and see, and ask others in your area. Also, of course look at the papers and see who is advertising. If someone advertises on a regular basis then the chances are that it is profitable.

One word of warning: to some, advertising in a newspaper gives the wrong message. In the NCH office we often hear people saying "if they advertise there, they can't be very good, can they?", or "it doesn't seem very professional". Bear these thoughts in mind when designing your ad.

Newspaper advertising (2)

This idea was included in Keith Egleton's talk on practice building at the NCH conference in 2004. He told his audience that he supplies his local paper with some 40 different adverts, and rings each week to tell them which to use. Not only does this result in a steady string of client enquiries, on a range of issues, but also it means that the newspaper has a stock of ads that they sometimes use to fill space that they have not sold!

Newspaper advertising (3)

They may not like it, but you might as well tell newspapers exactly where you want your ad to be. The right hand page is generally seen as better than the left, but you may want to be "connected" in some way to a particular section, feature or another ad.

Yellow Pages advertising

Following on from a discussion on no-shows (see 'Therapy section' p83), Joy Gower sent the following:

'The subject of no shows was most interesting, with therapists having their own particular way of dealing with them. It is not only therapists that have to suffer with this complaint though as one reader suggests because all businesses that rely on folk turning up on time suffer in some way or other.

I would however take exception to one therapist saying that Yellow Pages clients are the worst. Maybe where they live, but here in Norfolk, some of my very best clients have come from YP, and any new therapist will heavily rely on YP for the first year until they are established. For my part, YP has been brilliant, and my photo in there works so well, clients say they chose me because of my photo there, I look, apparently, like someone they could trust. I did get a professional photographer who is highly experienced in photo shoots to take the picture, but within the first few weeks of being in YP, it more than paid for itself and the clients were brilliant. I do not pay for advertising any more, as I find that source of clients was not at all successful, but having had quite a few articles in the papers, I get good clients from that, and with a strong belief in hypnosis as soon as they turn up. As for smokers, I have set up an arrangement whereby they call me 24 hours before they are due for their appointment to confirm. I tell them that I understand that some smokers get cold feet and are afraid perhaps, and I will understand that as it takes some courage to come and stop smoking. Good post hypnotics there and I don't get many cancellations that way, and if I do, they are good enough to cancel by phone well before the 24 hours. It is all a matter of what works for the therapist, but it is fascinating to hear how others handle this."

The effectiveness of Yellow Pages advertising seems to vary from area to area, although our own experience has been positive. It's power is decreasing with the ever increasing availability of the internet: but then again, maybe fewer people will advertise there, and hence you may be able to get a bigger share of a smaller market!

Where not to advertise

There is a simple rule as to where to advertise and where not. This rule will, of course, have exceptions, but in general it has been proven to work. The rule is this: *If you are asked to advertise, then it is usually not worth it.*

We would be interested to know whether your experience matches this rule. We have tried most things, including GP appointment cards, wall-planners, directories, videos and information booklets. None have produced a worthwhile return on investment and most have been simply an exercise in throwing money away.

Yellow Pages are likely to call when you set up your business and then annually to see if you want amendments. They are an exception to this rule, but even Yellow Pages advertising varies in its "pull" in different parts of the country.

Transferable skills

Most people who train as therapists have had a career previously. Few train straight from school or university and many have had lots of jobs, and/or lots of experiences that they can draw on in their role as therapist.

As an exercise, write down all the roles you have had in the past. Include non-work roles too, and childhood roles. Then list the skills that you developed in those roles. Finally, look at how those skills are applicable to the work you do today.

Some examples:

If you worked previously with computers, you may be able to achieve the following more effectively than others:

- monitoring your own progress using spreadsheets etc
- designing your own website
- relating to analytical type clients
- being organised

If you were previously a nurse you may find that you are particularly effective in these areas:

- relating to those in need
- understanding medical jargon
- linking with those in allopathic medicine
- working under pressure

Remember to consider all roles, as all will have given you some transferable skills that will help you to improve your practice.

Do something every day to attract new clients

Do something every day to attract new clients. Simple? Maybe, but it will test your creativity! One idea is to brainstorm a question every morning and write down at least 20 possible answers.

Ask whatever question seems uppermost at the time, such as "How can I get more clients?", "How can I improve my advertising?", "How can I encourage more referrals?"

Then choose one of the possibilities and act on it NOW.

Define your philosophy/mission statement

The phrase "mission statement" is often thought of as a corporate thing, but we would like to suggest that it is just as important for you, as a therapeutic practitioner. Some of you will probably already have been put off, but please persevere....

It is often said about goals that if you don't know where you are going you won't get there. Similarly, if you don't know what you are about, you won't convey this effectively to your target market.

Napoleon Hill called this having a "definite purpose". So what is your purpose? Why are you offering your service? What do you want for yourself and your clients? Are you enthusiastic about this purpose? What is the philosophy behind it? Does this fit with your personal philosophy of life?

These thoughts can then be drafted into the form of a mission statement, but even if you don't want to take this last step, thinking will bring extra clarity and enable you to convey your purpose more effectively.

Here at the UK Academy we went through this process and developed the statement:

'The mission of the Academy is to advance the professional practice of the therapeutic arts and sciences through the provision of high quality courses and excellence in the support of our students, members and associates while recognising that the needs of the public who receive the therapeutic services are paramount."

Behind this statement is our passionate belief in the power of the therapeutic process and the benefits that it can bring.

Record where your clients come from

A simple idea. So obvious everyone must do it. Yes? Do you? If so well done, because you will know what marketing works for you and what doesn't. If you don't, you are not alone. We hear this all the time. A therapist may say, "My Yellow Pages advertising doesn't work", so we ask, "where do your clients come from?" and they don't know. Unless you ask, you won't know, and unless you keep good records, you won't be able to see the patterns clearly.

What do your clients want?

A crucial factor in providing a service is providing what your clients want or need rather than what you think they should want or need. This idea reminds me (Fiona) of a time when I went into a shoe shop and asked for a particular shoe in a size 3 and was told they didn't have them, but would a size 4 do? Strangely enough, I wasn't impressed!

In therapeutic work however, clients are often vague about what they want, and sometimes unrealistic. For example, a client who attends for hypnotherapy to stop smoking may want the therapist to "do it for them", or a coaching client may ask for assistance in "making life better". So you have a role in helping the client to discover what they want and need and to educate them in how you can realistically assist in this.

This may all sound obvious, but it is our experience that many in the therapeutic field fail for just this reason: they offer something that does not fit with the client's perceived wants and needs.

So, we would encourage you to look at this. To ask yourself the tough questions, and if you are brave enough, ask others too.

Ethics

Always do right. This will gratify some people, and astonish the rest.

Mark Twain

Let's also add, and annoy some! As someone who works in a therapeutic modality you necessarily are in a position of trust with your clients. By consciously deciding to maintain a high standard of ethics, you will not only be helping your clients but also helping yourself. You are much more likely to build a successful practice that will last if you choose this route. We hear regularly of the complaints made by clients and many of the professional journals detail such actions. All of us are susceptible to spurious complaints, but how much wiser is it to ensure that your practice will always be demonstrably ethical.

New Year Resolutions

This piece is written primarily for the hypnotherapists among you, but can be adapted for any therapeutic modality.

As each New Year approaches, traditionally this is a time for thinking about one's life and planning for the future. Maybe by making New Year resolutions, or maybe just through a feeling of renewal and change that a new season brings. Are you maximising the potential for working with clients on these issues?

How about writing an article for this for your local paper? Many are short of copy after Christmas and would be grateful to receive your input. Smoking cessation adverts often work well at this time of year, as well as towards the end of January when you may be able to capitalise on those who have tried to stop at New Year, and failed!

Stress is also often high at Christmas, so anxiety related therapy is often needed soon after, as of course is weight control!

New Year Resolutions: YOURS this time

We talked before about what you can do in your practice to tap into the market of New Year's Resolutions, and as this time approaches each year, maybe it's a time to think about how you can use this time to make your own. In other words, this is a good time to make or review your goals.

- Where would you like to be one year from now?
- What would you like to have achieved?
- How much money would you have liked to have earned?
- How would you like your relationships to be?
- What about your health?

Now...... the big question....... How are you going to make this happen?????

Plan your steps, make your plans, and choose to realise your dreams!

New Year's Resolutions (3)

During the festive season give some thought to your New Year's Resolution: maybe resolve to increase your client base by 2% this year by trying one new marketing strategy each month?

Looking forward

City and Guilds have identified what they believe will be the top 10 jobs of the next decade. One of them is psychology. They state:

"A combination of factors leads us to the conclusion that the demand for psychologists will increase over the coming decade: (1) Life coaching as individuals seek to understand what their core abilities and motivations are and which occupations this should lead them to pursue. There is an incentive for employees to obtain such professional advice and employers to provide it. One factor driving this process could be the expansion in further and higher education and an over supply of graduates who are unsure which career route to follow. (2) Worrying trends in divorce rates, family breakdown, dysfunctional families etc and the need for professional counselling."

(see www.city-and-guilds.co.uk)

We would choose to interpret the word psychologist as therapist, including psychologists of course, but there is also so much scope for coaches, counsellors and other types of therapist to deal with the issues mentioned.

Are you maximising your ability to deal with these growing areas?

Being a workaholic

This article was originally sent out the day after a Bank Holiday. I (Fiona) had meant to send it actually on the Bank Holiday and then question readers as to whether they were reading it on a holiday, but I am pleased to say, I was so relaxed and switched off that I completely forgot! I spent all day knitting, sewing, walking and eating. Do you allow YOURSELF sufficient downtime?

If it frustrates you that they don't allow laptops on a Ferris wheel, you may be a workaholic.

Dr. Donald E. Wetmore

Most readers of Inspirations will be self-employed therapists. Being self-employed offers particular challenges to scheduling one's time, especially if working from home. How often do we get calls from potential clients who say that they can only attend at 9pm or at the weekend? It can be very tempting to say "YES!" (Wouldn't the money be nice?). But what about time and space for you?

I once knew a therapist who invented a client called Mr Potter, who was given regular appointments, just to give the therapist time to potter about and do her own thing!

Ethically keeping your clients

From Joy Gower:

Thinking about clients who come to the end of therapy, therapists will often say that is it, you do not need me any more and there can be some feeling on the clients part that they dare not return for any more therapy because it would seem a failure.

As we only ever heal, we cannot presume to heal everything and so often in life other issues turn up, so as therapists, should we not be encouraging the client to return at any time they need some more help in finding the resources they need at that particular time? Many clients have said to me that they do not like to come back as they think end of therapy is for good, and yet as I explain; if you go to the dentist and he or she say that your teeth are fine, do you never go again?

Perhaps to create more business in the future we could be setting up that expectation, that if they ever do need us, then we are available and will welcome them back. It maybe this "mind thing", that clients think they are "cured" and see no need to return, but if we want to be even more successful, why not mention that if the need arises, then that is what we are here for and we understand them.

I have yet to read a book that covers this topic, many talk about ending therapy as if that it final, and yet I continue to have therapy myself and could not continue as successfully as I do without it. It opens my mind further each time, and I see new insights after each session. I don't feel a failure, on the contrary, I feel even more empowered to do the job I feel so passionate about.

One young successful client told me he would be seeing me every now and again until I am 80. How is that for optimism? He knows that life is a challenge and is not naive enough to think that all will be well forever. So I have a client for life now, albeit very now and then.

Target markets

It is not unusual, when working with supervisees, for us to realise that therapists have no real idea at whom they are targeting their marketing. Start by considering your areas of expertise and how you work and then here are some questions that you might like to consider:

- What age of client will fit best for you?
- Is your style more suited to one sex rather than the other?
- What socio-economic groups are you best suited to work with?
- Do you have particular skills that can reach a particular sub-section of the population (eg non-English speakers)?
- Are there geographic areas that you could reach but have not accessed yet?
- Do you have an affinity with any special interest groups that could be a source of clients?

Please note these questions are designed to open up options and not limit you! It may be that you feel that your style is more suited to female clients in which case some of your marketing can be aimed specifically at women, but at the same time, you may consider how to develop your skills in working with men. Another example may be in terms of age: let's say that you are particularly skilled in working with young people who are lacking direction. Great, so market this, but you may also adapt this to work with older people who are feeling lost after redundancy or retirement.

Websites

For years we have talked about the importance of having a website in order to assist with the development of a successful and ethical practice. However, having a website and no control is not particularly useful. What we mean by control is that as much as possible you control and edit the content of the website. Studies have shown that a website that is updated regularly will generate more quality hits than those that are static.

We have heard of a therapist whose website was contrary to the code of ethics of her professional society. Because she did not have control of it, it cost her a lot of money to have it fixed.

So if you don't have control….. think about getting it!

For specific advice, email Shaun at shaun@ukacademy.org giving details of your site and the set up you have in place.

Monitoring your website

Many therapists have a website; however do most therapists know how effective it is? It never ceases to amaze us as to how many therapists simply do not know whether their website is effective or not. There are several ways to do this, the most obvious is to get some sort of matrix stats programme. This is generally available through your ISP. Also you can get Google or Alexa toolbar. These will give you a report on the relevance of your site as well as a report into who is linking to your site. Finally, it is essential that you determine where your site appears on the main search engines like Google, MSN, Yahoo and Ask.

How can you maximise your website?

Content rich website

We recommend that you have a website (of course!) that is full of content. Your potential clients want to know that you are an expert, that you are qualified, and that you can help them. Have some biographical details, and a picture. Look at other websites: what appeals to you? How can you model it?

Complaints

Not a very comfortable issue, but have you ever had anyone complain about you? This may be formally, or informally. Maybe they have just muttered that they aren't happy. Maybe they have cancelled a cheque, or asked for a refund.

If so, please be aware that you are not alone. If they are honest we would expect most readers of Inspirations to be answering "yes" to this question. Certainly all of the authors of Inspirations are willing to admit that they have had unhappy clients. In a busy practice this is inevitable and all you can do is your absolute best to minimise the problem.

This means ensuring that you offer an ethical service and that the fact that you are ethical is apparent. This means being clear and upfront about all that you do, about yourself, and about your therapy and its limitations.

Many of the complaints we hear about are due to a lack of information and explanation. We heard of a therapist who saw a client for three hours in the first session and then asked for two sessions worth of fees despite the only communication about session times and prices was to say that she offered a free initial consultation. All that was required was openness and a lot of unpleasantness would have been avoided.

The key is to be aware, to be open and to be prepared to learn. Listen to any grumbles and honestly ask yourself is there anything that you could and should be doing differently? Also be aware that you cannot please all of the people all of the time, and however hard you work at being a perfect therapist, you will not be for every client.

KISS

You probably know the acronym KISS. If not, it stands for Keep It Super Simple (there are a few variations on the SS bit). It means that simple is generally better than complex, but it isn't an easy balance. If describing your therapy to potential clients, how simple do you want to make it? For a start it will depend on how simple it actually is, but also, in order to have credibility, one must appear as an expert. What you are doing must be seen as involving skill and knowledge, otherwise why would they bother to pay you? We know that therapy does involve these things. We also know that it must be explained in language that the client understands, so that they do actually know what is going on and also so that they do not feel inferior.

Something to bear in mind whenever we are communicating, in writing, or vocally.

Design of Materials

Some time ago, Fiona attended a design workshop, and picked up lots of tips to be incorporated into our practice building courses. Here is just one:

The Four Principles of Great Design:

1. Alignment: every element on a page should have a visual connection with another element (either horizontally or vertically aligned, or both)
2. Proximity: the reader will see elements that are close together to be connected, and those that are physically separated to be unconnected, so you need to ensure that the elements that truly are connected are in proximity and those that aren't, aren't.

3. Repetition: without overdoing it, elements of your design (eg logo or bits of the logo) should be repeated throughout to create consistency.
4. Contrast: ensure sufficient contrast between sizes, foreground and background and fonts (if using more than one).

Staying power

Many people say that therapy is a difficult business in which to make a good living. David Newton has just sent us some interesting statistics from the Hypnotherapists section of the Bristol Yellow Pages. In 1993 there were 29 display ads, of which only four are still advertising. In 2002 there were 30 ads. In 2003 there are 30 ads, but 11 of these 30 are new. One can presume therefore that at least some, if not all of those who no longer advertise, no longer practice.

So what makes the difference between staying in practice and not? Here are a few possible factors:

- being proactive in building your business
- being professional in all respects
- committing oneself to the business
- being prepared to learn

If you have been in practice for more than a few years, may we ask you a question? What single factor has been most crucial for you in giving you staying power?

Staying power, continued

We had very little response from our readers to the question posed about how our more experienced readers have stayed in practice! Does this mean they do not know, or they do not want to share their secrets?

We strongly believe in sharing our secrets to build a successful practice. Isn't it in everyone's interests that our profession be strong? If the public see that therapists do not stay in practice, isn't it likely that they will negatively judge the efficacy of our work?

This from Jan Barton:

"In answer to your question of Practice Building I would say that my staying power has been a learning curve of the ups and downs, particularly in that I have learnt I CANNOT help everyone. I always give 100% commitment and energy to every session I give and I now tell my clients this and tell them that I expect at least this that back in return when it comes to doing the homework which I set them. My very gentle approach still remains, but I have learnt that sometimes I need to be more assertive in expecting something back. It has worked for me and most of my clients now come on recommendation, which I love. People often ring and ask what my success rate is, but as everyone knows if you are honest you never really know, but a recommendation must mean you are doing something right!

To sum up I feel that building a practice has been very hard work, tiring but hugely rewarding."

We wholeheartedly agree with Jan. Commitment and energy will translate into results, and results into referrals. Also, being honest with potential clients rather than quoting unreliable and improvable rates will improve your relationship with the client and hence success.....

From Joan Bower:

I am happy to share my own experience of how a practice can build up successfully.

I was a trained counsellor before I qualified in chiropody and found that the counselling skills really helped because any hands-on work creates an intimate environment in which people will often share their deepest concerns.

Qualifying in hypnosis purely for my own interest meant I didn't promote this service but when, in conversation people learnt of my training they wanted me to help them. Better the devil they know or something....

Seriously, from then on my practice has changed from mainly chiropody to mainly hypnosis with 90% recommendation. (Have now got several chiropodists working on my behalf)
As far as measuring this success goes, for a while I gave clients an outcome form which I was sending to a research project, also keeping a copy on my files.

I now always give out these forms and the ones I receive back are showing about 80-85% success although, of course, some don't find their way back to me.

If I have to give the main ingredient for success it is a genuine concern for your fellow man, woman. I remember being told a long time ago that research showed that regardless of how highly qualified people are the genuine concern is of the utmost importance!!

From Joanne Blah:

Even with one person making a dozen recommendations you may only get one client so building a business can be slow was based purely on recommendation. I have found many of my clients by talking at business lunches and speaking at ladies clubs, the more you talk to people the easier it for people to find out who you are and whether they feel you can help them. I have found brochures to be effective as I can leave them at different venues plus I can post them to all my callers, clients can pass them to friends and colleagues, plus mail outs can be effective. Yellow pages and newspaper advertising I have found to be expensive and has cost more than the return, however a small yellow page advert may let people know you are there!, Be prepared to work hard and I have found it can still sometimes take up to 3 years

From Joy Gower:

I am in my third year of practice, and my outcomes for success have exceeded my initial desires, and of course I believe in what Joan says.

Some say "be very good", but what does it take to be very good? Excellent training to start with, but also ongoing training, not only to keep up to date with techniques, but also to share with fellow therapists.

We can never know it all, and I am constantly surprised about how much I learn every time I read yet another book or go on a training session. I come away feeling even more inspired to do as well as I can for my clients.

To be a success, we must have the belief in ourselves first and know that we can make that client feel differently about themselves and the world when they leave you. After all, what they have is a negative belief about themselves, that is why they come to you, and you can call it a trance state they are in about that belief, so we need to de-hypnotise them from that belief.

I like Terry Watts' advice for building your practice and that is tell your client about an imaginary or real client that has successfully stopped smoking, or lost weight or anything else that you think may help. This gives them the idea that you are good, and also sells your other services too which they might not be aware of. Always remember that smoking clients think you only do smoking, and usually know someone else who you may be able help, and if they say so, give them a couple of your cards or leaflet. I have been surprised where my leaflets end up, in pubs, doctors, dentists and hairdressers. I was very pleasantly surprised to find my leaflets in a special rack in my hairdresser's right by the coffee table for all to see and have had many clients from that. I must admit it is horses for courses re the yellow pages as it was my main source of business for the first year, but get the ad right, and you will get many calls and people saying they chose you because of that ad. I think many people do look in the YP if they do not know any therapists or have been recommended, but obviously a recommendation is by far the best because they already come with that post hypnotic that if it works for Joe Bloggs, it will work for them.

I think the EZine Inspirations is so good to keep in touch with what is happening out there. Keep going, good therapists need this.

Develop your USP

Do you have a Unique Selling Point? If not, then develop one! It is one of the most fundamental elements of being successful in practice. There needs to be a reason why your potential clients choose to see YOU rather than a competitor.

Many newly qualified therapists struggle with this idea. It does take time to develop one's own style and confidence, but this needs to be a priority. There are schools out there who prefer to create students who are clones, and there are programmes which teach their students to "do it this way and only this way". This is not our philosophy.

So, what makes you unique? Of course, the word unique doesn't need to be taken literally here. Maybe you are unique in your geographical area, or maybe you choose to specialise in something that other people do too, but you make a feature of it.

Your USP may be an attribute you have, a clientele that you prefer to work with, a technique you use, a pricing structure, or something else. As long as it is ethical, then you are free to be whatever you want!

USP, a view

From Mureen Hunt:

Regarding the USP, how do people get feedback from their advertising - without putting (potential) clients on the spot? I'm good at finding out where people found me and have found that 'friendly and approachable' was my ad's selling point, as is 'past life with spirit releasing therapy' however that possibly puts some people off. I know that the people who ring me don't ring my friend (unless they are ringing around). Initially, I went through the countries yellow pages ads and took out what appealed to me and feel that my ad represents 'me,' however this next year, Yellow Pages have taken my words and arranged a fantastic advert for my third year, incidentally I feel that this ad also represents the client's expected results. With more competition, I need my ad to produce for more.

Problems?

There is an old adage that any problem can be seen as an opportunity. Perhaps also, changing the word "problem" to "project" can help the reframe.

So, if you have "problems" in getting enough clients, for example, reframe this into a project to be completed, with timescales, goals and action steps.

Modelling

"If you wish to know the road up the mountain, ask the man who goes back and forth on it."

Zenrin

I expect you remember when you were at school, and there was an absolute rule that you must not copy from someone else? Such a strong rule that most people are left with a strong injunction that copying is wrong. The concept is still around (appropriately), as adults in that we should not plagiarise, or even copy CDs. However, do you take this injunction too far?

NLP has the concept of modelling, and in terms of practice building, there is, in my opinion, no better way than modelling those who have succeeded.

Respond!

A supervisee of mine, newly qualified, and just setting up in practice, got a friend to ring round all therapists in his local area. He got another friend to email them. The results were fascinating! Many therapists just simply did not respond, and many more did so in such a way as to demonstrate either that they were desperate for the booking (on the phone), or conversely, that they did not care.

Elbow grease

Elbow grease is the best polish.

English Proverb

There just is no substitute for hard work. Manifest? Sure! But action is required too.

Don't leave the benefit till the end

It is important that advertising/marketing materials show the benefit to be obtained from your service right at the start. Many people make the mistake of detailing too much before showing the client what they will get. This process will vary depending on the medium you are using. For example, a practice brochure that is sent to enquiring clients does not need to emphasis benefit as early as, say, a newspaper ad, because the reader will already have an interest. An ad must capture the potential client's interest early.

Photo captions

Research has shown that photo captions are read far more than the body of an ad or article. Bear this in my mind: if you include a photo in your ad, put a really good caption that will grab your potential client's interest.

Your clients don't care about you!

As always, this statement is not an absolute, but there is a balance here that needs to be addressed. Your potential clients care that you are qualified, ethical, competent and are the "right person" for them. Your materials need to show this. We have often seen ads (and even websites) that exclude any mention of the therapist or coach. This is important, but it is also important to recognise that beyond this, you are not important. The client is not interested in meeting your needs!

Rent out leaflet space

There are differences of opinion as to the effectiveness of leaflet drops. However, one idea that can mean that you might as well try it is to print a leaflet with your details on one side. Rent out the other side to non-competitive businesses, perhaps eight boxes on an A5 sheet.

Newspaper article

Call your local paper (or a national) and ask:
"What would it take for me to have a really interesting article printed in your paper?"

Have your article ready.

Aiming

The odds of hitting a target go up dramatically when you aim at it.
Mal Pancoast

Marketing

Marketing is not something that just happens. It is a crucial part of your business and one that you need to devote TIME and EFFORT to. Consider yourself to be the marketing director of your business. You could even pay yourself for that role for so many hours per week!

Be yourself

I (Fiona) wish someone had told me to be myself when I first started in practice. I did not realize how vital a factor your own personality is, being a therapist, for years after I started. When I wavered from the ideas that I had been taught, although I felt that it was right, my conscious mind was telling me that I was getting it wrong.

You are your greatest asset! Use it. If you have issues that are blocking your progress, use your therapeutic skills and knowledge (including knowledge of who to consult) to remove them!

Learning

"I am always doing things I can't do, that's how I get to do them."
Pablo Picasso

What do your competitors do differently?

When first in practice, most therapists ring round their competitors, and look at their websites, with the purpose of finding out how much they charge. But much more can be gained from this process, and it need not be restricted to your local area. Now, we are not suggesting that you phone everyone in the country and ask for their brochures or we will all be spending a fortune on postage! However, websites can provide many and varied ideas for how you can develop your practice, and sometimes show you that you are doing the right thing already: good for your confidence!

To do lists

"Most "to-do" lists and their contents create more stress than they relieve because to a large extent they represent thinking and decision-making still undone. They have become reminders of guilt and

overwhelm, not sources of clarity or catalysts for productive action. Effective lists should be the result of appropriate and sufficient thinking, not salt in the wound of avoided decisions and conversations. "

Dave Allen

If money was no object...

If money was no object, how would you market your practice? You may wonder why I ask this. I ask because I have seen several examples of therapists deciding not to use a particular marketing tool because it is too expensive, without realizing that even though expensive, the return would still be good. Examples include deciding not to have an entry in Yellow Pages (in this particular case the therapist would have needed four sessions booked from the ad during the year to break even), and not producing quality brochures.

So, start by asking yourself this question, and then analyse whether it is your belief and value system that is holding you back rather than the reality of the situation.

Does a free initial consultation get you more clients?

Our feelings are that offering a free initial consultation at the beginning of one's career may be beneficial, when there is time for it. However, we have found that those who are coming for this are more likely than average to fail to show up, and to stop therapy early. Presumably this is due to commitment. However, there will be some good potential clients that you might lose if you aren't careful. What do we mean by careful? It's a question of how to answer when they ask "do you do a free initial consultation?" We recommend that you give them the opportunity to say that they can leave without obligation after 15 or 20 minutes if they do not want to continue, *or if you feel that you are not able to assist them.* This latter part does two things: it builds your credibility, and increases their trust in the fact that you have their well-being at heart.

What is your experience?

Does a free initial consultation get you more clients? Part 2

We had a wonderful response to this question, and here are some of our readers' thoughts! Opinions varied hugely!
From David Devere:

In one's early days at a new clinic, it is my experience that the more you do to raise your profile, the better. A well-publicised Open Day is often a good start. In no particular order, I detail below several discussion points.

I ensure that the receptionist only accepts bookings no more than one week ahead, thus not clogging up the diary. This saves thumb-twiddling between appointments.

My flyer is careful to mention that the free consultation is a 30-minute chat with no obligation and that no actual free treatment is given. I give an estimate or quote depending on the presenting problem.

I carry a temporary flyer which I pin up in reception when I have a 1-hour gap between appointments. "Today from 3 pm our Hypnotherapist is free to answer YOUR questions ... an informal chat ... David treats many conditions including X, Y and Z". The odd client does drop in after they've had their bones reset.

*Reassurance is often needed. "Who is this guy?" "Will I be forced to do something I don't want to do?" and the worst one – "Is it anything like wot I've seen on the telly?" This chat is the only chance for them to put a face to a name and is your only chance to sell your qualities as a therapist. At a very early stage I place a Berlin Wall of a dividing line between TV / stage hypnotists' activities and how a caring therapist will use the deeply relaxed state for the client's **benefit**.*
Nervous clients are encouraged to bring Mum / partner along too. This not only reassures them but provides me with an extra walking advertisement for my services.

*In the early days, if the client said she would go away and think about it or need to talk to her husband, I would politely leave it at that. In such cases they usually don't return (there is always an ignorant friend who will spook them by saying I'll have them clucking like a chicken). Nowadays I am learning to become a little bolder and I challenge them: "When I hear a client saying that, I feel that they do not have sufficient commitment to the successful outcome of their treatment. Success demands three things: time, my fee and your commitment." And if I really want to ram the point home, I let them know that I have a vested interest in maintaining my high success rate and am only prepared to work with those clients who do **not** expect me to wave a magic wand in just one session.*

In my experience, 2 out of every 3 free chats result in a booking. On balance, whilst becoming established this has to be worth it. Having said that, I look forward to the day when I can enhance my credibility and scarcity (and bookings) by withdrawing the free consultations. The day will come when my reputation alone will speak the volumes needed, and the free consultation will be a thing of the past.

From Jo Goss:

I was interested to read your comments on free initial consultations. This is something I do occasionally do, and I have found that they can sometimes be helpful. However, I don't offer them as a matter of course. My normal practice when potential new clients telephone to make an inquiry is to not only show an interest in what they need help with, but also to tell them something about hypnosis, and also give them the opportunity to ask as many questions as they want. Usually this results in a firm booking. However, just occasionally the enquirer may still be doubtful, or may not be comfortable talking on the phone, and if this is the case I then offer a 30 minute free initial consultation. I stress that they are under no obligation whatsoever to book any further appointments. I have only done this five times in the past 18 months, but in every case it has resulted in a new client, although one of these did stop therapy early.

When I do hold such a consultation I always allow time for them to turn this into a full fee-paying session if they wish. Only one of the five did so, and interestingly she is the one who stopped her therapy early. The others all chose to come back on another day. I had wondered if this might indicate a lack of motivation, and had anticipated cancellations or no-shows, but they all did turn up, and all went on to complete their therapy.

From Jan Barton:

I would like to comment on your question about initial free consultations.

I don't feel that free consultations are necessary or advantageous.

Whenever I speak to potential new clients I always give them the choice of receiving some information from me first by email or in the post or having a think about what we have discussed on the telephone. I stress that it is extremely important that they choose the therapist they 'feel' is right for them, particularly as they may end up sharing some of their very personal issues in their life. I give an initial 2 hour consultation (paid) and include in this some relaxation and visualisation so that they are fully aware of everything that is going to happen next time. I have developed this system as I find it takes away initial fears and gives them an opportunity to ask as many questions as they like and gives me the opportunity to gather lots of information which I can use in future sessions. Patients with deeply emotional problems will often 'use' this first session to just talk which is their choice, but if it is needed, then that's what they get. Of course the reverse may happen and they really don't want to talk much, so therapy may start straight away. Sometimes they have already 'moved on' merely from talking about and sharing their feelings and experiences which they might never have done before. I always tell them that if they decide at the end of this session they feel I am not the right person for them or they decide that hypnotherapy is not the way forward for them they have absolutely no obligation to book another appointment. I give them the choice to phone and make another appointment later, but I usually find they are keen to continue with the therapy as the fears have gone and they feel comfortable with me as their therapist. I think this is particularly relevant for the very nervous patients or for those who it has taken a great degree of courage to make the first step to changing something in their life. Since I have been working in this way (about 3 years now) not one person has failed to show for their appointment and resolutions to problems seem to have been slightly quicker.

From Gloria May:

I have never given a free first consultation. After all, even if I can't help with a client's presenting problem I am still using my expertise and my time. I think a free first consultation indicates to the prospective client that you are not a serious professional, and not confident in yourself or your work. If I am offered something 'free' it usually means there is a catch and I think an initial free consultation makes people mistrustful gives them the impression that they are being sold something rather than getting something they need. A bad idea, even for beginners - in fact, especially for beginners.

From Rachel Hastings:

With regard to the free session issue - it's worked very well for me. I don't get any cancellations or no-shows and have an almost 100% percent sale rate from this. I spend an hour, give the client a chance to start talking immediately about their issue, do a very small amount of pretalk about hypnosis, and give the client a 20-minute ego-strengthening session at the end. It never seems to fail. The only time a first session is not free is if the therapy is a possible one-session deal anyway, or if the person has a time-limited issue - big interview the next day. With regard to whether I would stop this in the future, I would only do that if I was insanely busy, but I may favor scheduling further out and starting a waiting list, rather than cutting the time on the free sessions - I haven't come to that point yet.

From Carole Ballantyne:

Just a couple of comments on the entry in Inspirations re a free initial consultation. I totally agree with the comment about the time factor - particularly if your Practice is only part-time and you are trying to see as many clients as possible over a shortened period.

I also think that it's a question of putting a value on your services, and that clients will have more respect for what you are doing for them if are expected to pay from the outset - which then leads on to a greater commitment and motivation on their part. However, the option of curtailing the first session without obligation seems to me eminently sensible and gets very neatly round this issue, for the reasons already stated in the ezine.

From Lyn Martin:

I do not offer a free initial consultation for several reasons.

1. My time is just as valuable the first session as it is with any subsequent sessions.
2. I probably work harder during the assessment and treatment planning stage than at any other time, so why shouldn't I get paid for it
3. I don't have time for 'chats' with clients. Many of my clients are very busy people who want to get on with the treatment to relieve symptoms and get on with living. I am also very busy, usually with a six week waiting list, so I want to work with clients as quickly and effectively as possible. The vast majority of my clients are referred by past clients, so I am confident that my work is effective.
4. Many of my clients only need one session! How would I make a living? Most people who come to give up smoking only need one session, as do most people with

*phobias - I saw a woman last week who was absolutely
terrified of driving. Even sitting in the driver's seat gave
her a severe panic attack. She was driven to the
appointment by her partner and she was very nervous.
At the end of a single session she asked him to hand
over the keys and she drove away quite happily. Even
adolescents suffering with nocturnal enuresis rarely need
more than two sessions.*

*For many clients I can complete my history taking, assessment
and treatment planning, followed by treatment in one session. It
would feel unethical to spend more time than necessary.*

*I can see why people feel that they might attract more clients
by offering a free initial consultation, but I prefer to ensure that
prospective clients are committed to working and making
changes when they phone for an appointment. So maybe I do
the equivalent of an initial consultation on the telephone.
Perhaps we need to define what happens in an initial
consultation before deciding if it is appropriate/ necessary or
not.*

What a range of opinions!

The race is not always to the swift, but to those who keep on running.
                                                    Anonymous

Charging appropriately

We were asked us to comment on charging. We firmly believe
that we should be appropriately compensated for our services
as therapists. We are aware that there is a tendency for some to
believe that as this is a vocation, we should not charge very
much, or even anything, and while, if this is your view, we
respect that, but we do not share it. The question is then: what is
"appropriate"? We have heard of therapists charging hundreds
of pounds for a session, sometimes when they have no better
(or even worse) qualifications and experience than other

therapists. This, we believe is unethical, and unsustainable long term.

We suggest that you find out how much the other therapists in your area are charging and pitch yourself somewhere in the middle, depending on your experience. We have also heard of therapists who charge more with the intention of seeing fewer clients for the same income. Again, this is a choice, but unless this is combined with some system of giving concessions to the needy or doing pro bono work, we feel this is depriving some people of the chance of receiving help.

Continuing what works

One of the most common marketing "mistakes" that we see is NOT continuing to do what works. If you find a marketing tool that makes you a profit (however small), continue doing it, until it no longer works!

Write out your marketing plan

The start of a New Year is often a good time to make a new start, and a new start is always a good time to plan. How are you going to market yourself during the coming year? We suggest that writing out a clear and detailed plan will help you not only to market effectively, but it will enable you to stick better to your plan, and to be clear about your goals. Also, write out exactly what you hope your strategies will achieve.

Making the most of opportunity

Opportunity is missed by most people because it is dressed in overalls and looks like work.

Thomas A. Edison

This quote reminds me of a therapist I (Shaun) met once at a conference who was complaining about a lack of clients. I asked what marketing he did, and he said "just Yellow Pages". I asked about his advert, and he said "I haven't changed it in years: I always seem to miss the deadline". I did not probe further, I didn't think it my place, but he certainly left the impression of being one of those therapists who seem to expect clients to simply drop from the skies!

There are plenty of opportunities, even simple things like the Yellow Pages, but it all involves DOING SOMETHING!

Geographic scope

Are you making the most of your potential catchment areas? This does not necessarily mean setting up separate clinics, although this is possible, but means looking at which areas you are advertising in. You can also see where your key competitors are, and you may well find gaps. People do travel for therapy, to see the practitioner they feel is right for them, but they won't know you are right if they don't know you exist!

Improving your service

If you won't be better tomorrow than you were today, then what do you need tomorrow for?

Rebbe Nachman of Breslov

Technology

Isn't technology wonderful? Except when it isn't! We recommend that therapists make the very best use of technology; for example, websites are now no longer a luxury but, we believe, a necessity. All your materials (brochures, letterheads, ads etc) should refer to your website and give an email address for contact.

However we mustn't forget that these things are not perfect. Only today I was reminded of this as the last Inspirations was rejected by someone's spam checker as it contained the word "sex". This was in the context of research looking at age and sex differences! Beware the Big Brother nature of spam checkers! This therapist who did not receive that copy of Inspirations would also not receive enquiries from clients who refer to sex in their emails, as many clients do even if sex is not their primary issue.

Listening

Hearing is one of the body's five senses. But listening is an art.
Frank Tyger

You may wonder why this quote is under the heading of practice building. The reason is that listening is one of the key skills that therapists need in order to be successful. Clients need to feel that they are listened to. We only need to listen (there it is again) to the stories of people who have problems with their doctors to recognize how important this is. I heard a radio programme which discussed complaints against doctors and a researcher commented that most complaints were against doctors who the patients perceived had not interacted appropriately with them (whether the complaint was specifically about this or not).

Also, remember that you must not only listen, but show that you are listening. The client needs evidence!

Self belief

"Your chances of success in any undertaking can always be measured by your belief in yourself."
Robert Collier

Do you believe in yourself ENOUGH? If not, why not do something about it? Maybe even try therapy? (Know any good therapists?)

Incoherence blocks flow

From David Allen's Productivity Principles:

"When there are ingredients in a system not aligned to its purpose, the whole mechanism is inefficient. Negative pressure

is created as energy gets dammed up at the blockage, and flow is diminished. An ineffective person on a team, a misaligned tire, the wrong tool for a job, and too many words in a sentence create static on the line and reduce productivity. "Get it together" is an appropriate admonition for maximum output and results."

Taking away

"In anything at all, perfection is finally attained not when there is no longer anything to add, but when there is no longer anything to take away."

Antoine de Saint-Exupery

What do you do that is interfering with the perfection of your service?

Self-confidence

"One important key to success is self-confidence. An important key to self-confidence is preparation."

Arthur Ashe

In therapy, this is an interesting paradigm. A successful therapist must have confidence in their ability and the efficacy of their therapy or the client will not believe. They must also, however, be well prepared, not only in terms of being ready with their interventions but also being ready to listen and empathise with whoever and whatever they are presented with.

Why do your current clients choose you?

In running our practice building weekends, and working as mentors with new practitioners, we have found that most therapists cannot answer this question. They are often so delighted to be getting the clients, that they don't even think to ask. Ask? Yes! Ask! How else are you going to know?

Once you know why they choose you over your competitors, you can build on these aspects, and/or work on the aspects that they do not mention. For example, they may say that they chose you because your Yellow Pages ad mentions your affiliation to a professional body. If however you spend a lot of space listing, for example, the conditions you treat, and no one says that is why they chose you, if may tell you something.

Complexity

Much of what sophisticates loftily refer to as the "complexity" of the real world is in fact the inconsistency in their own minds.

Thomas Sowell

Therapy isn't complicated, although clients often are. When training, we often find that this maxim holds true: once a concept is truly grasped and understood it becomes simple.

An important point though is that you don't want your clients to think that what you do is "simple" as to them it is likely to mean it has less worth. Remember it is only simple because of all the hours and hours of training and experience you have!

Gucci

The Gucci family motto is *"Quality is remembered long after the price is forgotten"*. How can you apply this idea to your practice?

Monitor conversion of calls into clients

Do you already monitor how many of the phone calls and email enquiries you receive become clients? If so, good, if not, you really should! It provides excellent information about how you are perceived in your initial contact with the client. This initial contact is incredibly important and is a factor that is often overlooked.

Your therapy room

The environment from which you work can have a profound effect on how happy your clients are, and therefore on how likely they are to continue with you and to refer friends etc to you. I (Shaun) once had a therapy session with a therapist whose room was small, grubby, untidy and noisy. She was wonderful and I cannot fault her interventions, but I did not feel comfortable to suggest to others that they should visit her. Conversely, I saw a supervisor who also worked from a small room but it was cosy, comfortable and felt very safe: she received several referrals from me.

How can you maximise your work space?

Your attitude

I (Shaun) was sitting in my office one day and thinking: 'What does it take to be a successful therapist?' Most of us have the necessary qualifications and skills, yet many of our colleagues are not as successful as they want to be. Then it occurred to me, the X Factor of successful practice is attitude. If you believe in yourself absolutely, you will get absolutely the best results, this is a common post hypnotic suggestion that I give to many of my clients in order to help them to succeed, and I now give the same suggestion to you.

How can you maximise your attitude for success?

Your beliefs

This article was originally written during the conference season for therapists, and it seemed an ideal time to mention attitude relating for success in practice. So often, we meet people who say "There is no money in therapy" or "it is impossible to make a full-time living as a therapist". It never ceases to amaze us that for people who are working to help empower people feel unable to empower themselves. Remember you get what you put out; your attitude can be the difference between being a hobbyist and a professional.

The phone

Ensure that only you answer the phone. We have called therapists and their phones been answered by children, lodgers, parents and of course spouses. (No pets yet to our knowledge but perhaps it's just a matter of time). It doesn't give a very professional feel when the first thing a client hears is "Darling, there's some woman on the phone for you!", or even worse if the person asks who you are. What does that do for confidentiality?

Your phone manner

It is important to remember that generally speaking the first contact a client has with you is over the phone. All too often we are distracted when we pick up the phone, the radio playing in the background, our minds on other things, or worse still being in a generally bad mood, all effect how we sound on the phone. As a policy, we would suggest that you do not pick up the phone unless you are in the frame of mind you would be in if the person was sitting in front of you.

Word of mouth

At the 2005 NGH Convention in Marlborough, I was once again impressed by how open people are with information. At a private meeting for Certified Instructors, one of our number was talking about the importance of word of mouth referrals. The secret of word of mouth referrals, other than to be good at what you do, is to give clients more than they expect.

Networking

I (Shaun) have been thinking since returning from the NGH International Convention that one of the things that therapist do not do well is network. I make a point of meeting at least 12 new people at every conference I attend. Very often these associations can be beneficial both personally and bottom line. How can you begin to network more with your colleagues?

Feedback on networking

From Joy Gower:

I agree wholeheartedly in regards to networking. Many people really do dislike the idea of having to contact people and make relationships with a view to getting work but it acts twofold

Most of the people I have talked to in the past who have networked and have given up doing it have done so because they felt they did not get business straight away. It simply does not work that way. Networking is all about raising your profile in your area, and getting known amongst the people you meet at events.

It works in just the same way as starting out as a therapist. You may think you are really good and that you have been trained well but in reality people have to get to know you and much of the work we can get is from word of mouth.

I have to admit that some of the network events I go to, including Chamber of Commerce makes me think, "here we go again" and you have to have the confidence to just walk up to people and introduce yourself, but one thing is in your favour. People love hearing about hypnosis, and anything to do with the mind because there is still mystery surrounding it, so the first reaction when you tell people what you do is of curiosity and great interest. Think about the poor souls who have to say they are accountants! They are great people usually, but it is not of much interest really unless of course you are desperately searching for an accountant.

Mostly everyone I have ever spoken to at networking events wants more information about hypnosis, and has many questions.

Since persevering with networking events, I have been asked to speak at numerous events, have gained many clients and made some nice friends, so it is worth making the effort to put your name about. My goals at the beginning of my career were to get a high profile and be known as one of the best in my area. I like to think that I have achieved that now and I know that it is because I made the effort to network. Apart from creating more business, you really do learn so much from other people, and you never really know who you are going to bump into and where that may lead to.

How committed are you?

"How committed are you? There is a remarkable difference between 99% and 100%!"

Vic Conant

Mistakes

List your mistakes, review them regularly, share them with colleagues: we can all learn from each other. Maybe you would like to share yours through Inspirations?!

Difference

I was sent (by Val Hird) some lovely silly quotes which I will use sparingly here. Here is one, with a serious message behind it:

We could learn a lot from crayons. Some are sharp, some are pretty and some are dull. Some have weird names and have different colours but they'll have to live in the same box.

Do you have any issues with difference that are interfering with your success?

Effort

Keep the faculty of effort alive in you by a little gratuitous exercise every day.

William James

Don't you think this idea translates well to practice building? Do a little something every day....

Talk it up

"Personal honor is the mortar that holds the bricks of life in shape. If your sense of honor is stronger than your mood, you can never give in to negative feelings."

Author Unknown

Something we discuss with many newly qualified or struggling therapists is to "act as if" your practice was as you would want it to be, by doing this you are able to use the full capacities of the unconscious to manifest the future you want as opposed to what you do not want. How can you utilise this in your practice today?

Will and fear

To succeed, the will to do so must be stronger than the fear of failure.

Referrals

Why not get together with other complementary practitioners in your area and set up a group referral scheme?

Waiting for success

As therapists I'm sure we have all known colleagues who seem to expect clients to fall out of the sky into their consulting room. This is not likely! I could just sit in my garden with my arms out-stretched waiting for a passing plane to drop a bag of money down to me by parachute. It could happen, but it isn't very likely….

If you wait for success to happen, it won't. It's something that you make happen or it can't be called yours.

Success is a lousy teacher

Success is a lousy teacher. It seduces smart people into thinking they can't lose.

Bill Gates

Need

Is your NEED getting in the way? If you really need to convert each prospect into a client, they are likely to pick this up as a negative when deciding who to go to. Time to trust that if you are doing the right things, your practice will build and no one client will make or break it!

Educate your market

They need to know you are there and that you can help them! So often clients appear when they have seen something about therapy on TV and say "I didn't realise anything could help my problem". How can you help them to discover that you are there?

Ask

Ask friends, family and colleagues for their opinions on what you do, how you do it and your materials. Ensure they feel they can be honest and get them to put themselves in the position of a client first. I (Fiona) remember when I was first in practice NOT doing this because I was worried that I would be criticised! I soon got over that one and have learnt a lot.

Capitals

When Writing An Advert Avoid Starting Every Word With A Capital Letter. It Looks Odd And Creates A Feeling of Discomfort In The Reader. For a headline you can capitalise the keywords. Eg: Stop Smoking in One Session using Hypnosis.

Make your clients feel special

Make them feel special, but don't over do it! I (Fiona) regularly buy clothes from a particular catalogue, but if it wasn't for the fact that I really like their products more than their competitors I would take myself off their mailing list. Why? Because they constantly send me letters saying I am a GOLD level customer or some such nonsense. I don't buy much! I know they must be sending this to everyone: I've even had thanks for my good custom when I haven't bought anything. In making people feel special we need to be sincere.

Free advertising

To find places where you can advertise your services for nothing, enter "free advertising" and your area into Google.

Heroes

"Heroes are not there to be copied. They are there to inspire us to be different and better."

Unknown

A slightly different "take" on the usual modelling idea. The key is that we can all take bits from heroes, but we all need to find our own way to be ourselves.

Reducing risk

Some therapists ask for money up front for sessions, sometimes asking for payment for a block of bookings. We recommend that you simply charge by the session at the end of the session, thus reducing the perception of the risk to the client of "wasting money".

A business card idea

This idea came from a colleague in the USA. It is to put a magnet on the back of your business card so that clients (or potential clients) can stick them on their fridge (or filing cabinet perhaps). One thought though: if you do this, do remind your clients not to put them in their wallets or the magnet could interfere with credit cards!

Magnetic cards (2)

Following our tip about putting a magnet on the back of your business cards, Lyta Humphris from Plymouth emailed to say that she produces magnetic cards for smoking clients with tips on how to remain a non-smoker. The idea could easily be extended for weight control clients, and I'm sure many other issues. All you need is imagination.

New format for business cards

You can now get cds in the shape of business cards. What could you do to take advantage of this way of marketing? You could record an introduction about you; explain what hypnotherapy is and what it helps. The benefits of what you offer and any USP (Unique Selling Point) like a free consultation. You could hand these out at fayres and public speaking engagements. You could give your clients your usual cardboard business card and then give them a cd version to give to someone they know could benefit from your help. You could even have an instruction on the cd to listen to it once and then pass it on to another person. This could be a great form of viral marketing for you.

Tip provided by Steven Harold
http://www.MarketingTherapists.com

Increase your network with your business card

They say we are never more than 6 people away from anyone in the world. This may or may not be true but even if a small percentage of this were true that would still mean that you have a connection to thousands of people. Whether you are a new or experienced hypnotherapist, when was the last time you handed your business cards to your network requesting that they hand them out to their network? Why not give everyone you know (who agrees to do it) 6 cards each and ask them to hand them out to 6 people they know. If you only have 10 people who agree to do this you will have increased your network by 60.

Tip provided by Steven Harold
http://www.MarketingTherapists.com

Increase your network with your public and group talks

The most cost effective way to get your name out to your community is to go out and do talks on therapeutic subject which you are expert in. In the early days of building up my practice, I (Shaun) would often have 2-5 library or service group talks planned each week. A service group is something like the Masons or the WI places where people meet to network and develop. If you do this, very often the library or group will take care of all of the marketing for you so all you need to do is turn up. Of course bring goodies to the talk with you like brochures, business cards and CD's. I assure you that doing this will pay huge dividends for your practice.

How to ask for referrals

Easy! But often therapists feel uncomfortable with this. All you need to do is to give a brochure or card at the end of the session and say "Share this with your friends if you think they could benefit"

MOTIVATION

The magic word?

You have probably heard of Earl Nightingale. One of his ideas is of which word is the most important in the English language. This particular word can be seen as underlying everything about how we live, how we progress, whether we succeed or fail, whether we are happy or otherwise. Do you know what the word is? It is ATTITUDE. One's attitude determines everything!

Why people don't set goals

Do you set goals for yourself? If so, do you do so in every area of your life? Another time we will look at the benefits more specifically, but here is a list of reasons why people might choose to miss out on this productive habit:

1. they aren't serious in their endeavours
2. they have not accepted responsibility for achievement of the task
3. they have low self-esteem and so do not believe in their capacity to fulfil the goals they would set
4. they don't know why they should
5. they don't know how
6. fear of rejection/criticism
7. fear of failure

Do any of these apply to you? If so, what are you going to do about it? Maybe nothing, or maybe something that might just make a big difference!

Wisdom

Aristotle is quoted as saying that wisdom comes from an equal amount of experience and reflection. Perhaps we could add knowledge too. To be wise therefore means knowing, experiencing and reflecting. As therapists we often strive for wisdom, particularly as many clients are looking for this to inspire them, and maybe we concentrate too heavily on the knowledge and experience part of the formula.

Do you allow yourself adequate time to reflect on what you learn and what you experience?

Do it now!

"Do not wait; the time will never be 'just right'. Start here you stand, and work with whatever tools you may have at your command, and better tools will be found as you go along."

Napoleon Hill

When dreams become goals

"Vision is the art of seeing the invisible."

Jonathan Swift

We all have dreams, but how many actually become goals; goals that can be achieved? Perhaps the first step is to have a vision of the dream, not as a dream, but as potential reality. To move away from the "impossible" feeling to a "well, maybe...." feeling.

The next crucial step is to write down your vision. This makes it into a goal. Then plan the steps that need to be taken to reach it. You may need countless intermediate goals, but in doing this you give yourself the second element that is required, and that is a feeling of hope. With a list of intermediate goals and action steps, that feeling of "well, maybe..." can grow and fuel your action with a feeling of expectation.

Finally, by taking action and achieving these intermediate goals, you find a feeling of fulfilment: the third factor required to convert a dream into a goal.

(Adapted from the work of Steven K Scott)

Let me give you a simple example (Fiona writing). My son, Greg, has struggled with his spelling. He doesn't appear to hear words in the same way as other people, so writes them the way he hears them. This is being worked on, but in the meantime, at weekly spelling tests at school he regularly feels upset at his "failure". This came to head last week, so this week I suggested that he could set himself a goal to get 10 out of 10 on Friday.

He looked at me in astonishment. "That's impossible!" he said. He then said he didn't want to set the goal because if he didn't achieve it he would be upset. But he recognised that he would be upset anyway! I assured him that if he believed it to be impossible, it would be, but maybe....

We worked on his spellings, dividing them into syllables and linking them to other words (eg parent became "par" (he loves golf!) and ent). Within 20 minutes he got 9 out of 10 right. He then had hope.

By practising during the week he found fulfilment, and so his belief in the possibility of achieving the impossible goal grew.

Thomas Edison

Everything comes to him who hustles while he waits.

Thomas A. Edison

Thomas Edison conducted more than 10,000 experiments in his quest to develop a light bulb. That shows persistence! After he succeeded he is reported to have said that he was bound to succeed then as he had run out of things that didn't work!

The future

"Plan for the future, because that is where you are going to spend the rest of your life."

Mark Twain

Many of you, reading this, will be therapists who spend considerable amounts of time going back in time with clients, looking for sources of problems etc. However, this can distract us from what is important: the future. So, whatever you do with

54

your clients, and yourself in your own therapy etc, remember to dream, set your goals and think ahead!

The Prime of Life

Be on the alert to recognize your prime at whatever time of your life it may occur.

Muriel Spark

Please read this quote in conjunction with the piece in the therapy section on beliefs (p91). Do you have a belief about when you were/are/will be in your prime, or when you should be? Maybe have a re-think!

Maybe you could be in your prime every time your age is a prime number: whether that is 19, 37, 53 or 71!

Goal Setting

As we've discussed before, setting goals is a vital part of being successful. But how do you do so effectively? Here are the elements required for good goal setting:

1. Develop a desire
2. Develop a belief that it is possible to achieve
3. Write it down
4. List benefits
5. Define starting point
6. Set deadlines
7. Ascertain obstacles
8. What extra info is needed?
9. Who can help?
10. Plan
11. Visualise
12. Never give up

How about using this procedure to develop a goal of goal setting on a regular basis??

Finding opportunity

The door of opportunity won't open unless you do some pushing.

Anonymous

And you have to know it's there to push at it!

What opportunities are you missing because you don't notice the door, or don't push at it?

Humour

Angels can fly because they take themselves lightly.

G.K. Chesterton

I (Fiona) was reminded today of a woman overheard complaining at a conference that "I came here to be educated, not entertained!" I had been in the same sessions as she had, and while some parts had been hilariously funny, I had also learned a lot. Doesn't humour help the learning process? In fact doesn't humour help with most processes? Of course, humour should be used appropriately and tastefully, but even in a therapeutic setting it has a place.

We'd be interested to hear any examples you may have of times when humour has assisted you in your therapeutic role, or of course, if you feel that humour has no place in our work.

Humour continued

We are grateful to Jo Goss for the following feedback:

"On the subject of humour, I have found that it most definitely has a place in hypnotherapy, provided it is used appropriately. I've found it particularly helpful during initial interviews when clients often feel rather nervous; if I tell them about hypnotherapy in an interesting and enjoyable way rather than giving them a dry lecture they are more likely to relax quickly, and also to remember what I've told them. It is also very helpful in establishing rapport.

Its use during the actual therapy needs caution. Clients obviously need to feel that their issues are being taken seriously. However, its use shouldn't necessarily be ruled out completely. One of the most effective sessions I had was with a client who was suffering from lack of confidence and self-esteem, caused largely by her childhood experiences. I said something silly - I wish I could remember what - and she suddenly burst out laughing, and went on and on. Hysteria? Maybe, but it released a lot of tension, and from then on she improved rapidly and is no longer receiving therapy.

I'm a firm believer in using anything that helps the client, and humour, used appropriately, can help significantly."

In discussion with several readers, it appears that the use of humour is generally perceived as useful. A couple of people referred to laughing "accidentally" when a client was relaying their issues. In both cases, the effect was positive, despite the initial perception on the part of the therapist being that they had made a mistake. Can you think of any examples? Or, conversely, examples of when the use of humour has backfired?

Failure

Success is going from failure to failure without loss of enthusiasm.
Winston Churchill

It may seem a strange title for a piece on motivation, but failure is critical to success. Failures teach us important lessons, and also, to never fail means to never be pushing very hard!

What is important is how one handles failures. In fact some of our readers may object to the use of the word, especially NLPers. However, for our purposes, let's call a spade a spade. Can you learn from your mistakes, from criticism, from disappointment? Or do these things make you want to run and hide? I (Fiona) must admit that I have a tendency to the latter, that I work hard to overcome. I remind myself that it is ok to hide for a little while, then I process the information and adapt if I believe there is a benefit to be gained from this.

It can be hard to do. When is criticism valid and when should it be discarded as incorrect? I was criticised for being disorganised at an event. I know that this was untrue as everything was as it should have been. However, the criticism taught me that I had not conveyed this organisation adequately and so this understanding will affect my behaviour in future. Also a supervisee told me that a client had criticised him for not wearing a tie while seeing clients. Now that, in my model of the world is an invalid criticism.

To avoid criticism, do nothing, say nothing, be nothing.

Elbert Hubbard

Do you love what you do?

Do you know what the greatest test is? Do you still get excited about what you do when you get up in the morning?

David Halberstam

What does a New Year mean to you?... a fresh start perhaps?... maybe you've just had some time off.... do you feel excited about your therapy work for the coming year? If so, brilliant! If not, perhaps it's time to look at why, and what can be done to bring that excitement back.

Expectations

It is a funny thing about life: If you refuse to accept anything but the best you very often get it.

Somerset Maugham

How do you feel as you read this quote? Do you expect the best? Are you to happy to accept less than the best? Do you strive to offer the best?

I (Fiona) was prompted to think about this following a series of terrible service in shops in the week after Christmas. Maybe I was just unlucky, or maybe the universe was telling me something! Maybe I am getting fussier! Whichever, I have resolved to expect the best, and more importantly to up the level of service that I offer to my clients. I know how much I care about my clients, but do I demonstrate that adequately?

Open Mind

The mind is like a parachute. It doesn't work unless it's open.

Unknown

Yours and your client's!

Planning

"Don't wait - plan ahead folks! It wasn't raining when Noah built the Ark!"

Jan Ruhe

Sometimes planning can be a really therapeutic process, and it creates its own motivation. Just think of how much fun it can be to plan a holiday!

Use this idea when planning your schedule.... set goals.... and have fun with it!

Brains

I not only use all the brains that I have, but all that I can borrow.

Woodrow Wilson

You are probably used to people who think that they shouldn't have therapy because getting help is a sign of weakness. Do you at any level? Do you think you shouldn't use other people's knowledge and wisdom too? That's what mentors, supervisors, coaches, colleagues etc can do for you amongst other things!

Key objective

"Fixing your objective is like identifying the North Star - you sight your compass on it and then use it as the means of getting back on track when you tend to stray."

Marshall Dimock

Being Open-Minded

Be open minded, but not so open that your brain might fall out.

C Scott Giles

This quote was used by Scott to describe his ideal attitude for a person living with cancer. That is to be open-minded to the extent that the person can accept possibilities, but not to the extent of gullibility.

Enjoying life

'The really happy man is one who can enjoy the scenery on a detour"

Anon

This quote caught my eye, following watching an SAS programme on TV one evening, where members of the public are put through exercises to see if they are "tough enough". The contestants were walking through the Namibian desert in what to me would be intolerable conditions, and I found myself wondering whether they would still be able to see the beauty of the scenery of if the physical and psychological toll would prevent this. I have no answer, but what about life in general, and the therapy life in particular?

Can you, as a therapist, let yourself be content, at a deep level, even when circumstances aren't ideal? Or when dealing with the horrifying stories our clients often bring? Keeping an awareness of all the positives can help us to keep going.

Life is like a mirror

Life is like a mirror. If you frown at it, it frowns back. If you smile at it, it returns the greeting.

Herbert Samuels

Mirroring is a common technique in rapport building, and some forms of therapy see the therapist as a mirror in which the client can see themselves reflected. The image is a powerful one, and can be used, not only for our clients, but for our own growth, as therapists and human beings.

Courage

Courage does not always roar. Sometimes, it is the quiet voice at the end of the day saying, "I will try again tomorrow".

Anon

Courage (2)

Courage is not the towering oak that sees storms come and go; it is the fragile blossom that opens in the snow.

Alice Mackenzie Swaim

Leadership

I was watching a film yesterday called "the Core". I won't give you a full critique of the film, but one line struck me as rather insightful. The glamorous female lead was wanting to captain the space shuttle, but was told that she could not as she was so successful in everything she did, and that "you're not really a leader until you've lost". Later on (stop reading if you don't wish to know what happens!) she suffers set backs and becomes the leader (successfully of course).

How does this apply to us as therapists? Perhaps we can be seen as temporary leaders for our clients as they change. In which case, it makes sense that we have to have "lost" in order to be able to lead them. This doesn't necessarily mean, however, that you need to have suffered in the same way as every client. There are schools of thought that suggest, for example, that only those who have been abused should work with the abused, and we would not agree with this injunction. The important thing, perhaps, is to recognise that your own "failures" or "weaknesses" or "losses" can help you to be a more empathic and therefore more effective therapist.

"It's always been done that way"

The most damaging phrase in the language is: 'It's always been done that way.'

Grace Murray Hopper

Continuing the theme from the Practice Building section, it can be truly motivational to recognise that you can innovate. As a therapist you have a real opportunity to be yourself in your work, to bring to it your own style and to make a difference by being different.

Wishful thinking, or....?

Stop the habit of wishful thinking and start the habit of thoughtful wishes.

Mary Martin

Do you imagine your future as you want it to be? Do you do so regularly and clearly? If not, why not? Never underestimate the power of your unconscious mind to manifest for you.

Change

"Only in growth, reform and change, paradoxically enough, is true security to be found."

Anne Morrow Lindbergh

Witnessing the motivation of others

If you ever find yourself in the position of lacking motivation, either generally or specifically, one of the best ways to change your mood is to watch or listen to others expressing their motivation. During the International Train the Trainer Programme, Shaun and I felt privileged to witness the demonstration of huge motivation on the part of the students, firstly to achieve their qualification, and secondly to become successful trainers. Therapy fields can often be full of apathy, and it is easy to allow this to bring us down. It is so important to remember the opposite and allow the positivity to bring us up too!

Each day

Every new day begins with possibilities. It's up to us to fill it with the things that move us towards progress and peace.

Ronald Reagan

The Inner Team

Unfortunately, Kashmir Sidhu was not well enough to present at the 2004 NCH conference, but I (Fiona) delivered her material (hope I did it justice). Her key idea, on the issue of motivation, was to develop an Inner Team, with different knowledge and skills to motivate them. The team includes the concept of modelling, reprogramming, positivity, incorporation of all senses and enabling.

Confidence

"Confidence doesn't come out of nowhere. It's a result of something…hours and days and weeks and years of constant work and dedication."

Roger Staubach

Are you one of perhaps the majority of people who think that you either have confidence (maybe related to activity), or you don't? Many believe that confidence will grow alongside competence, but what about if the two were separated?

True confidence comes from a deep inner belief in worth. So work at it!

Rain

If you want the rainbow, you've got to put up with the rain

Jimmy Durante

Thank you!

God gave you a gift of 86,400 seconds today. Have you used one to say 'thank you'?

William A. Ward

And what are you using the other 86,399 for?

Teaching pigs to sing??

Never try to teach a pig to sing. It wastes your time and annoys the pig.

Mark Twain

This is an interesting variation on the "I can do" principle which I like to encourage my clients to believe in. However, there are limits, and that is ok!

Perspective

I'm looking forward to looking back on all this.

Sandra Knell

A lovely way to keep perspective when things are tough.

Energy

On our professional coaching course, two students gave a presentation on motivation (an excellent presentation, may I add). One of their primary points was to link the idea of motivation to energy, and to demonstrate how part of the process of a coach motivating a client is to share positive energy with them. The opposite side of this coin is to avoid being depleted of energy when working with a client who is down.

If you do not have people in your life who will give you an energy boost when you need one, it may be time to find them!

Avoiding burnout

We have heard many therapists expressing fears of attracting too many clients and thus getting burnt out. This is often given as a reason for not marketing themselves, but is, of course, a valid concern. Melissa C. Stöppler, M.D., gives five tips for surviving burnout:

1. take inventory: put pen to paper and get a clear list of all responsibilities, resources and options
2. pare down
3. delegate
4. pamper yourself
5. know when to seek outside help

Inspiration

Inspiration exists, but it has to find you working.

Pablo Picasso

Music

Music can be one of the best instant motivators, and while many use this on a regular basis, it is often something that we do with little thought. Dr Damon, president of the National Guild of Hypnotists plays "I feel good" by James Brown when he starts his keynote lectures. The same music was on in his office when Shaun and I visited one year. What a wonderful anchor!

If music is not something that you use regularly, specifically to adapt your mood, then you should try it! As I (Fiona) write this, I have some music playing that was in the charts when I was a teenager. It is powerful and strong in both melody and lyrics and I am instantly transported back to the teenage feelings of determination that this track conjured up for me then. (Incidentally I can use it much more productively now!)

Doing your bit

I am only one, but I am still one. I cannot do everything, but still I can do something. And because I cannot do everything I will not refuse to do the something that I can do.

Helen Keller

You cannot help everyone, but your therapeutic work is SO important to those that you do help. Remember that.

The gifts of life

Each day comes bearing its own gifts. Untie the ribbons.

Ruth Ann Schabacker

When you feel overwhelmed

"Nothing is particularly hard if you divide it into small jobs"

Henry Ford

I was reading a book on education last week which discussed the concept of "hard", and referred to a conversation between a father and son about Airfix kits. The son insisted that the "harder" kit was not really harder, because all he had to do was the same thing (stick bits together), but for longer. How many tasks that overwhelm us could be looked at in this way?

Seeing more

If you look at zero you see nothing; but look through it and you will see the world.

Robert Kaplan

Frogs and bugs

"Frogs are smart: they eat what bugs them"

Sign outside a Garage in Nashua, New Hampshire

Why this sign was there, we have no idea, but it really says something! What bugs you? What do you do with it?

Metaphorically eat it, ie deal with it? Or do you let it carry on bugging you?

Be who you are

Be who you are and say what you feel because those who mind don't matter and those who matter don't mind.

Dr. Seuss

How many of us can honestly say that we live to this?

What you do

"Ability is what you're capable of doing. Motivation determines what you do. Attitude determines how well you do it."

Lou Holtz

How about maximizing all of these?

Happiness

Happiness is when what you think, what you say, and what you do are in harmony.

Mahatma Gandhi

Success

Success is going from failure to failure without loss of enthusiasm.

Winston Churchill

Success and work

"Dictionary is the only place that success comes before work. Hard work is the price we must pay for success. I think you can accomplish anything if you're willing to pay the price."

Vince Lombardi

Keys to success

"I don't know the key to success, but the key to failure is trying to please everybody."

Bill Cosby

How can you utilize this idea for both yourself and your clients?

Pure inspiration!

Learn as if you were going to live forever. Live as if you were going to die tomorrow.

Mahatma Gandhi

Is giving everything enough?

You give 100 percent in the first half of the game, and if that isn't enough, in the second half you give what's left.

Yogi Berra

Common sense

I won't claim this as original but I cannot remember where I heard it. But someone very wise once said that the average person has huge amounts of common sense as they haven't used any of it yet. Do you use yours?

The courage to dream

'The world lies in the hands of those who have the courage to dream and take the risk of living out their dreams - each according to his or her own talent.'

Paulo Coelho

Do you have the courage to dream? Is the world in your hands?

Positive mental attitude

A strong positive mental attitude will create more miracles than any wonder drug.

Patricia Neal

Don't complain

"If you don't like something, change it. If you can't change it, change your attitude. Don't complain."

Maya Angelou

You can be great (if you aren't already of course!)

Keep away from small people who try to belittle your ambitions. Small people always do that, but the really great make you feel that you, too, can become great.

Mark Twain

I hadn't seen this quote before, but it sums up our intention in producing this ezine. We want you to be great. We want you to offer a great service to your clients. We want you to promote therapy as a great thing, for the benefit of the public and the profession. You can do it!

Playing

We do not stop playing because we grow old; we grow old because we stop playing

Anon

Do you still play? Can play be a part of work too?

Climbing mountains

Mountains cannot be surmounted except by winding paths.
Johann Wolfgang von Goethe

Maybe this quote can be useful for when the weather is getting nicer so that you can imagine a pleasant stroll on a mountain. And isn't it nicer to take the winding path than try to go straight up?

Does it last?

People often say that motivation doesn't last. Well, neither does bathing: that's why we recommend it daily.

Zig Ziglar

Motivation: …..and you

Have you ever wondered why some clients improve and some do not? Even in cases where the symptomology is almost identical and the intervention is identical some improve and some do not. I would like to offer you a thought about being motivated. Are your clients and are you? Are your clients clear about where they are going and what they want exactly? The same question for you with regards to your outcomes and goals. Research has shown that clients who are motivated are much more likely to achieve their therapeutic outcomes than those who are not. Additionally, to increase this level of success further, if the therapist is motivated he/she can assist their clients to be more successful and if the therapist is motivated he/she can even assist clients who are not motivated into being so. So what does all this mean, simply put we need to be aware of how ours and our client's motivation effects the therapeutic process. These questions have been asked as a precursor to Fiona and Shaun's book *Motivational Hypnotism*. In this book the dynamics of motivational theory are examined and shown how they can be put into practice to make the therapeutic intervention more successful than perhaps what was previously attempted. Whilst this book is geared towards hypnotherapists, there are very useful bits of information for the counsellors and psychotherapists in practice as well.

Dreams

We can all dream and be creative. In an instant a two year old can turn a cardboard box into a spaceship a submarine, a time machine. We have all been two year olds at least once. We are all creative, we are all dreamers.

Frank Dick

How can you utilize this idea for both yourself and your clients?

Dreams 2

Why have dreams if you are not prepared to keep appointments with them?

Frank Dick

Dreams 3

More from Frank Dick on the subject of dreams:
Your dreams are like a rolling sense of destination. They are the other side of the horizon, a never-ending story. To reach them you must see limits as perceptions, not as realities. Dreams, then, are milestones on a journey without a final destination. Don't stop dreaming.

Why?

"Why cry if you can laugh? Why wait if you can act? Get out there - make a difference!"

Unknown

How can you utilize this idea for both yourself and your clients?

Desire

"Desire is the key to motivation, but it's the determination and commitment to an unrelenting pursuit of your goal, a commitment to excellence, that will enable you to attain the success you seek."

Author Unknown

How can you utilize this idea for both yourself and your clients?

Goal vs desire

"A goal is not the same as a desire, and this is an important distinction to make. You can have a desire you don't intend to act on. But you can't have a goal you don't intend to act on."

Tom Morris

Now

"If you don't push yourself to the limit, how do you know where the limit is?"

Unknown

No regrets?

"The only things in life you ever really regret, are the chances you didn't take....to hell with the consequences!"

Author Unknown

Portrait of an achiever

From Marcia Tillman:

Failed in Business - Bankruptcy, 1831
Defeated For Legislature, 1832
Failed in Business - Bankruptcy, 1834
Sweetheart - Fiancée Dies, 1835
Nervous Breakdown, 1836
Defeated in Election, 1838
Defeated For U.S. Congress. 1846
Defeated Again For U.S. Congress, 1848
Defeated For U.S. Senate, 1855
Defeated For U.S. Vice President, 1856
Defeated Again For U.S. Senate, 1858
ABRAHAM LINCOLN
ELECTED PRESIDENT OF THE U.S.A., 1860

"You cannot fail . . . unless you quit!"

Being you

You are the best in the world at being who you are. Don't ever try to be someone else; just be better at being you and you'll always touch the mountain top you reach for.

Optimism

Optimism is essential to achievement and it is also the foundation of courage and of true progress.

Nicholas Murray Butler

Own it

If you're proactive, you don't have to wait for circumstances or other people to create perspective expanding experiences. You can consciously create your own.

Stephen Covey

All too often we attempt to avoid the strategies that motivate us; we should embrace these rather than repel them. So whether you are motivated by towards or away from strategies, use them for your own best future.

Good examples?

If you can't be a good example, then you'll just have to be a horrible warning.

Catherine Aird

An amusing quote, but one with something in it! Firstly it is part of our role to be good examples to our clients, of such things as boundaries and other ethical issues. Secondly, what about those people in our lives and in our clients' lives that cannot be viewed as good examples? We all have them. Perhaps we can make the most of such relationships to ensure that we, and our clients, know exactly what we do not want to be.

Motivation for your work

What motivates you as a therapist? Consider your motivational strategy - are you intrinsically or extrinsically motivated by your work? By this we mean are you doing what you are doing because of something inside of you or something from outside of you. It is important to recognise that an internal driver is preferred for the work we do. If you can model that for your clients you can help them to be more self reliant.

Flying

You must be prepared to get out of the comfort and security of the nest if you are to learn how to fly

Frank Dick

Plagiarism

Plagiarism saves time

Seen on a billboard outside Hooters in Nashua

Now we are NOT recommending plagiarism, but what about modeling? Look around for role models who embody the

73

qualities (perhaps of motivation) that you aspire to. How do they do it? What could you incorporate into yourself? There is no point in reinventing the wheel!

Changing your mind

The only man who can't change his mind is one who hasn't got one.
Edward Noyes Westcot

Self-discipline

Sometimes it is hard to motivate oneself due to a lack of self-discipline. Maybe you have a tendency to stay in bed too long, or eat too much, to procrastinate or one of many other habits which get in the way. One way to think of this is to tell yourself to be just a little better than the average person would be. This idea can motivate you to just that little bit more positive action which can break a habit!

Key attributes

Identify key attributes in your field, know you can develop them in yourself, and go for it!

Waves

You can't stop the waves, but you can learn to surf.
Unknown

Focus

It's not a question of whether to focus, but on what to focus.

You are focusing all the time, as long as you're conscious. The challenge is to direct that focus where you want, when you want. Eliminating mental distractions, clarifying intentions, and developing steadiness of concentration are master keys to creative success.

Future pacing for yourself

How often do we forget to use our professional skills for ourselves? Future pace, 18 months into the future and then work backwards to ascertain what it will take to enable you to meet that goal.

The truth

"If we all worked on the assumption that what is accepted as true is really true, there would be little hope for advance."

Orville Wright

Miracles

In order to be a realist you must believe in miracles.

David Ben Gurion

Doesn't this sum up our work nicely? Realistic and sometimes miraculous at the same time! What a wonderful job we do!

Key to failure

"I don't know the key to success, but the key to failure is trying to please everybody."

Bill Cosby

Earning

"We will receive not what we idly wish for but what we justly earn. Our rewards will always be in exact proportion to our service."

Earl Nightingale

Utilisation

Whenever motivation is lacking, utilise the things and people that you find around you. At the time of writing this, there was beautiful blossom on the tree outside my window. This raised my mood and reminded me of the beauty and positivity in the world that my work strives to enhance. What is there in your environment that can inspire you?

Obstacles

"Obstacles are those frightful things you see when you take your eyes off the goal."

Henry Ford
Founder of Ford Motor Company

Is life hard?

When I hear somebody sigh, 'Life is hard,' I am always tempted to ask, 'Compared to what?'

Sydney J. Harris

It's scary

Everything that is worthwhile in life is scary. Choosing a school, choosing a career, getting married, having kids--all those things are scary. If it is not fearful, it is not worthwhile.

Paul Tornier

THERAPY

The meaning of being non-judgemental

In the world of therapy, we often read of the need to be non-judgemental, but what does this really mean? Why is it important? How can it be achieved?

As human beings, we are naturally judgemental. In fact we are judging things around us constantly, assessing for danger, monitoring our own behaviour and ensuring our "position". It is an automatic process to judge another person, when we first meet them, and even with someone who we have known for years. We judge their appearance, their behaviour, their demeanour. So how can we ask ourselves to be non-judgemental? The answer is that is a question of what you do with that judgement and the reasons for reaching it in the first place.

Let's give some examples:

A new client arrives at your door. He is dressed in women's clothing. You WILL react to this fact in some way. If this were to produce a negative reaction within you, then the process of being non-judgemental involves putting this negative feeling to one side, recognising it as a feeling of your own and inappropriate to therapy, and continuing to engage in a therapeutic process with this client. Being non-judgemental does not mean that you have to go the opposite way and positively judge. Later, you can explore your reasons for feeling as you did and maybe learn something about yourself, or perhaps just recognise an old button that has been pushed.

Another client arrives with broken fingers. You enquire politely and he tells you that he got drunk and beat up his "best friend". He laughs as he tells you. Some therapists would use the idea of being non-judgemental to avoid this. They might think "I must be non-judgemental therefore I must show him I am not judging him". But, most of you, presumably would judge this behaviour as wrong. So, how can you convey that thought, but still not make the client feel that he is being looked down on, or "told off"? The best way is to draw the client into stating that what they did was wrong. You can often achieve this by the usual questioning techniques. You can then help him to recognise that it was his behaviour that was at fault, not himself, and so aid the therapeutic process.

Clients are used to being judged. They are, for the most part, used to receiving conditional approval. If you can be non-judgemental, while having your own feelings and beliefs, you are giving them the safety that they need to examine their own behaviour. Positive judgement is a type of collusion and can be as damaging as negative. You are not there to approve of your client. A possible exception to this is in the coaching relationship where the coach positively champions the client's behaviour, but in a particular way. The client needs to feel safe, and being non-judgemental, helps provide this.

So, to summarise. Being non-judgemental means accepting the person, but not necessarily their behaviour. However, it also recognises that that behaviour is their choice and in recognising this, the therapist can learn about their own process and deal with it, keep it out of the therapy or choose to refer on.

Unconditional Positive Regard

Last time we talked about being non-judgemental. Coincidentally, a few days later I (Fiona) read a letter in the August edition of The Psychologist about Client-Centred Therapy. One of the core conditions as expounded by Client-Centred therapists is Unconditional Positive Regard, which is akin to being non-judgemental. The writer states

"...unconditional positive regard is impossible in any human relationship. Most people with severe mental health problems have been treated badly, dislike themselves and are often unlikeable almost by definition. Genuinely likeable people probably don't need help."

Let's have a look at this; I was certainly rather disturbed when I read it!

To say it is impossible suggests a misunderstanding of what it is. Likewise to imply that UPR is the same as "Liking" shows a lack of understanding. Showing UPR does not mean that you like a person. It means that you are aware that the person is a human being with good points and not such good points, and that they are a product of all their choices and experience. Just as being non-judgemental does not mean agreeing with behaviour and choices, neither does UPR. Rather than ramble on, let me quote Carl Rogers:

"When the therapist is experiencing a warm, positive and acceptant attitude toward what is in the client, this facilitates change. It involves the therapist's genuine willingness for the client to be whatever feeling is going on in him at that moment, - fear, confusion, pain, pride, anger, hatred, love, courage, or awe. It means that the therapist cares for the client, in a non-possessive way. It means that he prizes the client in a total rather than a conditional way. By this I mean that he does not simply accept the client when he is behaving in certain ways, and disapprove of him when he behaves in other ways. It means an outgoing positive feeling without reservations, without evaluations. The term we have come to use for this is unconditional positive regard. Again research studies show that the more this attitude is experienced by the therapist, the more likelihood there is that therapy will be successful."

I would agree with the writer of the letter if he had "we cannot always show UPR", but it is an ideal to strive for, and, I believe is often really rather easy to achieve.

Many of you who are reading may not be working with "people with severe mental health problems", but I wonder if those that do would agree that they are often "unlikeable by definition"? I have worked with some in my time (and know others) who would fit the category of severe, and the fact that they have been badly treated and dislike themselves, doesn't, in my experience lead to them being unlikeable.

And finally, to say that "genuinely likeable people probably don't need help" is almost laughable! For you, as a therapist, this would mean that virtually all your clients are either unlikeable or are not in need of your help! And what about us? I have had therapy, as have many of you, possibly. I think I am quite likeable. I know a lot of the people who are receiving this personally and I rather like most of you!

So, I wonder why this letter writer feels as he does? I don't know, but I do know that I will continue to strive to both feel and demonstrate an unconditional positive regard for my clients and I am sure that I will continue to like most of them too.

The TOTE Model and Therapy (A Road Map to Success)

Many times therapists of all types wonder how a client goes about engaging in the behaviour that the individual has come in to be consulted on. Often times, client explanation can be woolly at best, so we offer you the following model to assist you in determining how a client does what he/she does.

This model was first developed in *Plans and the Structure of Behavior* published in 1960 by George Miller, Eugene Galanter and Karl H Pribram. **T.O.T.E.** stands for Test, Operate, Test, Exit which is a sequence based on computer modelling. We know that many therapists will be uncomfortable with the computer analogy, but from a behavioural perspective this is a nice model which can be implemented in order to effect change.

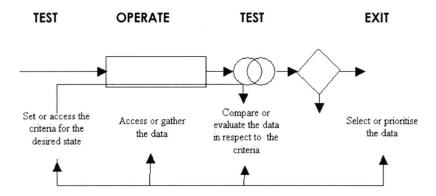

The first TEST is a trigger for the behaviour, in other words this sets the behaviour off. "What is the first thing that needs to happen for you to know it is time for you to do X?"

The Operation is how the client runs through his or her behaviour. "How do you do X specifically in steps?"

The second Test is established to determine whether the person has completed the strategy. "How do you know you have finished the behaviour?"

If the behaviour has run its course, then the client will Exit the strategy. If not the client can run through the behaviour over and over again until they reach the get either a positive or negative Kinaesthetic feeling at the end. It is feelings that tell us when we conclude a behavioural strategy as opposed to a logical assessment.

The implications of this model is clear, if we can help clients to affect a change in any of these steps, we can help the client to break the negative behaviour and perhaps help them to install something more positive and beneficial to replace what has been removed or altered.

Difference

Following on from the research article quoted above, I thought I would pose a few questions about working with clients who are "different" from you. I don't intend to answer the questions, I am hoping that you will ponder and answer them for yourself.

Do you have any issues working with people who are different from you in any of the following ways:

- Age
- Sex
- Race
- Religion
- Socio-economic status
- Education

- Physical attributes
- Politics
- Attitude

Do you give consideration to issues that people who are different from you in any of these ways may have in working with you?

Are you able to discuss any potential issues with your clients?

Do you have somewhere to take any issues that arise for you or them? eg supervision or own therapy

If you do not have issues with any particular differences, what is it about you that makes these differences ok?

What is it about you that causes any difference issues to be issues? What is it about your experience, your beliefs, your values, your own self-esteem?

"The Safe Space"

One of the key requirements for therapeutic change is the creation of a safe space for the client to explore, understand, and act. So what does a safe space mean? Here are some elements, both psychological and physical that we believe can contribute to the creation of a safe space:

- the client needs to feel accepted
- the client needs to feel heard
- the client needs to feel that it is ok to verbalise anything
- the client needs to feel it is ok to feel what they feel
- the therapist needs to be truly comfortable with the client experiencing whatever they experience
- the therapist needs to be able to demonstrate this
- the client needs to know that confidentiality is absolute (subject to the requirements of the law and supervision)
- the physical space needs to be secure. This means practically secure, ie there will be no interruptions, and also psychologically secure

- cosiness can often represent security, as can comfortable chairs and warm colours
- a clinical environment will often represent (maybe unconsciously) places of discomfort (maybe linked to authority)
- the therapist needs to dress appropriately in order to assist the process of the client feeling safe
- self-disclosure from the therapist needs to be used only to assist the client with their process
- touch can be used to assist with the process, but it is exceedingly tricky to get this right. In general we recommend an avoidance of touch unless you are 100% sure of yourself and your client in this respect
- music can help the client to feel safe, but others will find it distracting
- some clients may be distracted by views from windows, or sitting facing bookshelves, but others may prefer to have "somewhere to look"
- some clients may prefer to sit on the floor or cushions, but for others this may feel very unsafe
- the therapist needs to be aware of aromas in the therapy room and how different clients may react

As can be seen from this list (from which we have probably missed some obvious things?) there is a lot of individual difference. So, we will finish this section with a very basic, obvious suggestion that is often forgotten:

ASK THE CLIENT WHAT THEY NEED!

Dealing with no-shows

All those involved in therapeutic work have times when clients don't show up for their appointments. In the beginning, many practitioners find this disheartening and feel upset and maybe even that they have "failed". It is important, however, to recognise that this happens to everyone. You need to be able to understand the possible reasons, decide clearly what immediate action to take and then to act further if you feel, on reflection, that there is something you could have done differently.

Let's look at each of these points in turn:

1. There are many reasons why someone may fail to turn up:

   - it may be your fault (and we put this first as it is often the presumption!).
   - they may have forgotten, or changed their minds
   - they may be unavoidably detained
   - they may have got the date or time wrong

2. Whichever of the above is the case, it is helpful to know. So you could call or email to ask. They may well then rebook. If you don't call, they may be worried to call in case you are upset by them.

3. If you find that you are at fault, then you can make amends, either with them or for future clients. However, remember that NO therapist is ideal for all clients.

If you find yourself overly affected by no-shows, this may be something that you can look at. Maybe it is pressing a button of being under-valued, or not respected? Or maybe it is making you doubt your competence? Whatever you discover, look on this as a good learning process which will make you more effective in the future.

Many therapists have a clause in their contracts that stipulate payment must be made if the client misses an appointment without appropriate notice. We feel that this is a good clause to have, but insisting on its compliance is harder. Some ask for a deposit which will cover this eventuality. However we have seen cases of therapists becoming, in our opinion, too "heavy", by sending letters from lawyers to demand payment.

Perhaps it is better to write off a debt, and maintain good will? After all, the client may be in a position to want further therapy later, or refer you to others.....

No shows, continued

Here are some ideas offered by our readers:

From Jan Barton:

"Just a comment about "No shows". In my early days I used to feel disappointed, guilty and angry having sometimes for maybe having spent a lot of time preparing a session to find they don't show up. I now find that this is a total waste of energy and, as you say, happens to everyone. Wherever possible I have both a home and a mobile number and I telephone after 15 mins from the appointment time to "see if they are OK" bearing in mind they had an appointment with me at ....o'clock. I am always pleasant, as being angry only makes them defensive. I then ask them "what they want to do", giving them to opportunity to say I will ring when I find my diary, feel better or whatever excuse they give. Sometimes they have genuinely forgotten and are very apologetic. But don't be surprised if they make another appointment and don't turn up to that either. One guy said to me that "didn't I realise that was part of his problem, that he could not get up to make a 9 o'clock appointment!" He had decided on the appointment time, not me. Reasons are many-fold, some just plain 'porkies' and some really are not ready to 'move on' and don't have to bottle or courage to phone and explain and find it easier to just do nothing. Some get the wrong day, even when you write it down for them. What's that saying?

I always confirm initial consultation appointments in writing with a clause that provided I am given 8 hours notice there will be no charge and even then I will be understanding in certain circumstances, but you don't have a hope of pursuing 'no show fees' without a great deal of stress and aggravation. Hanging on to the anger or whatever you feel only damages YOU and I now deal with it by writing an initial letter stating that I was disappointed, concerned or whatever was appropriate for that person that they did not let me know that they would not be able to make the appointment and I then ask them for half the fee, 'which I am sure they will find reasonable". If this does not get a response I send a further letter stating that I would be pleased to receive a donation in whatever amount they deem reasonable for missing an appointment made payable to the Hospice that I work for. I thank them in anticipation, but state that should they decide to ignore my letter then I leave it on their conscience. It gives me closure and I don't give it another thought as I value myself, my time, my work and would rather give to someone else."

From David Botsford:

"With regard to "no-shows", a good idea is to send out a short letter with appointment card and map immediately the appointment is booked. This letter should briefly mention what you are going to do in the session to achieve the solution the person desires, thus maintaining the person's interest in attending. The appointment card reminds them of the time and date. The map helps them find you. (All these cut out many of the reasons for no-shows.) If the problem of no-shows is getting particularly bad, then it is good idea to ask for the person's credit card number and expiry date at the time of booking, explaining that it will not be charged until the time of the appointment, and that a fee is payable for non-attendance. It is a good idea to do this even if you don't have the capacity to process credit cards (the client doesn't know that). Although not every client will give these details, most will. And once you have their credit card details, you *always* get 100% attendance, without exception.

The clients who are most likely to turn up to an appointment, to co-operate fully and to pay without a problem are those who come to you by referral (either from someone they know whom you have already helped or from some health professional). Much worse are those who come as a result of seeing your paid advertising. The very worst are those who come from looking through the Yellow Pages."

We would disagree with the idea of asking for a card number if you can't take them: what would happen if they attended and wanted to pay that way?

From Jo Goss:

"I was particularly interested in your article in this edition on dealing with no shows. I have so far had only one, my very first client, and I found it a very discouraging experience. She had already had two sessions, and seemed to be progressing well, but at the third session I hit the nail on the head, and this brought about an abreaction. She was still feeling a bit emotional when she left. Imagine how I felt when she failed to turn up the following week. I thought I must have really misjudged the situation, and nearly gave up on the spot! I was uncertain whether or not to contact her, but I was concerned about her so I did so. In this instance at least, it was definitely the right thing to have done. She had, at the time, a drink problem, and had overslept. She later told me that had I not contacted her she would have been too embarrassed to come back, but that following the previous session she had, in fact, found a huge sense of release, and was very keen to continue her therapy. She has been attending regularly ever since, and is now doing very well. She has stopped drinking, and as a result is regaining her confidence and self-esteem. On the subject of payment for the cancelled session, I had intended to let it go, but she insisted in paying in full.

A related problem is that of clients who cancel at the very last moment. I would normally request half the session fee in such instances, but if there is a really good reason such as an accident at home or a sick child then I waive it. However, I find that some clients who do this have decided that hypnotherapy is not for them, but are too polite to say so, and that a return call prompts them to be more honest. This has happened three times so far. If a cancellation fee is due I do request payment, but if the client does not send it I do not pursue it further. I just write it off as a bad debt. From my own point of view, I think my problem as a new therapist is that of confidence. If a client is disappointed I feel that I have somehow failed, and worry that I am not good enough. However, I'm fortunate in that I have an excellent supervisor who, at my last session spent a lot of time helping me to put things in perspective and regain confidence in myself and my abilities. I can't stress the value of supervision too strongly! "

From Pam Segal:

"I was interested to read the piece in Inspirations about no shows. Until three months ago I had the same problems as every other therapists but found a method of taking a deposit which has worked well for me, in fact since I have started to use it about three months ago any client who has had to cancel has given sufficient notice and I haven't had a single 'no show'.

I use the Hypnotherapy Contract which I took from the NCH website, but have added two clauses of my own which are as follows:-

Cancellation with less than 24 hours notice unless in a case of extreme emergency will cause the client to be liable for the full cost of the session.

With regard to the above the client will supply a signed cheque in the sum of £40 prior to the first chargeable session. This cheque will be held by the therapist and will not be cashed unless the client cancels an appointment with less than 24 hours notice under circumstances which do not qualify as an extreme emergency and makes no contact within the following 24 hours to offer an explanation. The client will also be liable for any bank charges they may incur by cancelling any cheque payable to the therapist under these circumstances

*I always take the cheque on their first paying session, explaining that although I am sure that **they** wouldn't dream of cancelling without notice or good reason that some people do and I have to treat all my clients equally! I also explain that I don't care whether they cancel the cheque or not as the bank charges for doing so will be roughly similar to the cost of a session and I promise to return the cheque/shred it in front of them on their last session. So far all my clients have been pleased to do this and I haven't had to cash a single one of the cheques.*

I don't know if this would be of interest to any other members, but so far it has worked like a dream for me!"

A final word on this subject (for now!) from Chris Holmes:

"With regard to no-shows: all this talk of contracts, clauses, warnings and threats to chase fees in the event clients don't arrive - far be it from me to criticise my colleagues, but this really isn't rapport-building, is it? Yes, it's a tricky problem; this last August was particularly bad for me, with almost a thousand pounds-worth of business that was booked in not actually arriving, or postponing. But I cleared this one with myself ages ago. It's going to happen. You should expect it, and build it in to your overall practice management. Yesterday, one of my clients postponed and the next one didn't arrive. I spent the time doing my accounts for the last six months, which I enjoyed catching up on. It's self-hypnosis, folks: "She hasn't arrived? Great, I can go to the bank, and pick up some stamps while I'm at it!" I deliberately don't allow myself breaks or lunch hour during the day. I book clients in back to back, right through the day. So if someone fails to show, "Great, I can have some dinner!" Or take a break. Pay some bills, get my hair cut, whatever, just make good use of the time. Income-wise, don't expect everyone to turn up. I still had a strong August, because I don't bank on all those appointments materialising, and I make great use of the time created when they don't show up. Notice how I put that? The time created, not wasted. I never chase payment, or threaten to. Damages rapport. I work hard to make sure I have more clients than I know what to do with, expecting roughly a fifth of them to not show, cancel or postpone. Doesn't bother me a bit.

I never ask people to sign contracts or agreements - rapport is your agreement. Not only that - I accept all cheques on trust. When people hand me their guarantee card, I wave it away "I never bother with those!" Remember, this is at the end of the session, the client's still in trance - this is a dynamite suggestion, what are they going to think? "Well, I don't know if it's worked, but this therapist's bloody confident, he's accepting all cheques on trust!" Let me tell you, folks, I've accepted thousands of cheques on trust: none ever bounced, and only five have ever been cancelled later. Total cost to me so far, for this dynamite suggestion to hundreds of successful clients? £275 over three years. Well worth it. Did I chase the cancelled cheques? Yes, at first. Did I get anywhere? No, of course not, I just got all upset! Then I decided to take the long view. Now it just makes me smile. So few people prove to be dishonest, when someone is, it just reminds me how wonderful and honest everyone else is - because they could all have done that, couldn't they?"

The Consistency Principle

From James Malone – Certified Hypnotist, New Jersey, USA

"The problem of clients not showing up for their appointments is one that bedevils not only hypnotherapists, but also other types of appointment based businesses as well. An article by noted social psychologist Robert Cialdini in the annual Mind/Brain issue of Scientific American offers a practical suggestion to alleviate this difficulty.

Cialdini is well known for his research into the topic of influence and persuasion. In the aforementioned article he touches upon several key principles in the persuasion process including what he defines as "consistency." Simply put, this tenet states that asking for a public commitment related to some behavior or belief, even a minor one, greatly increases the odds of future compliance with a related request. He cites the example of a restaurateur who lowered the no-show rate at his establishment from 30% to 10% by having his receptionist change just two words during the reservation process.

Previously the receptionist would ask callers to "please call if you have to change your plans." By changing the phrasing of this request to "will you please call if you have to change your plans?" and then pausing briefly to allow for an affirmative response, the no-show rate dropped dramatically. This effect was attributed to the value most people place upon being *perceived as consistent in the social setting, even when interacting with a stranger.*

Besides the obvious application with booking appointments, the consistency principle could have additional applications in the hypnotherapy practice. For example, how about just asking clients up front as to whether they are fully committed to doing whatever it takes to get their desired change? One hypnotherapist I know of here in New Jersey who is also a lawyer actually made official looking contracts for his clients to sign related to the various issues clients see him for, pledging their intention to succeed. Adds a bit of drama and intensity to the work and makes for a great post-session souvenir too."

Beliefs

If a Plant's Roots Are Too Tight, Repot.

Gardening headline, The New York Times

We loved this headline when we saw it reproduced on a website about beliefs. A great metaphor for the constriction and restriction that beliefs can produce. Much of our work in therapeutic areas can be seen as relating to beliefs, and maybe a particular area for work is beliefs that are instilled in childhood and not re-evaluated. All children are "told" in one way or another what to believe about themselves and about the world. It is an important process. If children are told that "cars are dangerous", this, to them is no different than being told "people are untrustworthy" or "women should be subservient", or "if you are bad you will go to hell". It is merely a piece of information which they store and act upon. They do not have the capacity, as small children to differentiate and so it is vital that they act upon what they are told and not check it out for themselves. But most of us would probably like them to check out the other pieces of information and decide for themselves whether they are valid.

Many people grow up with beliefs instilled in this way, and do not get to the point of re-evaluation. Maybe then their "roots are too tight", and by an encouragement to re-evaluate, they can be "repotted". It is important to stress that this process of re-evaluation may result in the same beliefs, but if so, then they belong to the person, rather than having simply been "swallowed whole" from someone else.

Let's look a little more about the beliefs that people grow up with about themselves. Children are given messages, either directly or indirectly, with good intent, or not, about who and what they are. They are likely then to either live to those messages, or rebel against them, neither of which may be the most appropriate way for that child/adult to be.

An example: two children are told by their teacher at the age of 8: "you are hopeless at maths". Maybe they are told once, by a generally good teacher who is having an off day and loses his temper. Maybe they are told it repeatedly by a teacher who has problems of his own resulting in a need to denigrate his pupils. One child hears this and (unconsciously) processes this and creates a belief "I can't do maths", which sticks and results in him failing maths right through his schooling: he never even bothers to try: what would be the point?

The other child hears the message and thinks (consciously or unconsciously), "who is he to say so? I'll show him!", and so strives harder and harder and eventually gets a PhD in maths. A good result? Maybe, but is this motivation the most appropriate for an adult? To be showing his teacher from years before that he was wrong?

Finally there are those beliefs instilled about how one "should" be. Are these any more appropriate?

Encouraging clients to write

There is a huge potential benefit for your clients if they can be encouraged to write. The amount of encouragement required will vary from those who need none to those who wouldn't write if you paid them. The amount of benefit will also vary, dependent on many factors but perhaps critically on how free the client feels to really let go when writing. Here are some examples of how/what a client may write:

- a letter of apology to a deceased friend/relative
- details of how they were mistreated or abused
- an expression of their emotions (anger, love, isolation...)
- lists of who and what they are and are not
- stories of dreams, wishes, or of the past
- diaries or journals
- poems

If possible, clients can be encouraged to disregard such things as grammar, spelling, "getting it right". Splurging can be very effective: creating a direct link between mind and paper or screen.

Some clients prefer to use paper and pens, sometimes using colours. Others may prefer to type. If creativity helps then drawing can be utilised too.

It is also necessary for them to consider the security of anything they write, and need to realise that writing a letter does not mean sending it (necessarily). Burning the writing, or tearing into tiny pieces can add to the therapeutic process if appropriate.

More on Creativity

Last time we wrote about encouraging clients to write. This brought to mind another creative idea that can lead to interesting revelations from the subconscious that can be used within any therapeutic modality.

Many of you will already have tried this technique, but maybe you, like me, forget about it on a regular basis! It is a very simple technique, and however reluctant the client there is usually a good result. All you do is give the client a piece of blank paper and a selection of coloured pens or crayons, and ask them to draw their place in the world. (At this point in reading, you might like to stop and do this drawing for yourself).

When they have done so, you ask them questions about their picture and encourage them to interpret. For example, use of colour can be of interest, as can the size of figures and who and what are included and excluded. Other factors such as intensity of the drawing and relative positioning can indicate unconscious processes at work.

It is good to allow the client to do as much of the interpretation as possible, but it is ok for you to offer some possibilities as long as you phrase it in such a way as to not be "telling them" what their picture shows, but asking if it might.

Motivational work

Following on from the piece featured in the Practice Building section on the City and Guilds (p15), let's look at the coaching part of their idea. Many of you will be therapists whose work is primarily based around dealing with current or past issues and problems. It is clear that people's motivation to rid themselves of these is in order to have a better future, but many therapists miss out on the opportunity of working directly with the person's future when issues are resolved.

We have seen many references to a process of work whereby an issue is dealt with, perhaps by resolving past emotion, developing resources or making behavioural changes, all of which are fine, of course. There may then be some future pacing to develop a belief in the resolution, but how much better would it be for the client if you were then able to work with them to integrate their changes and to help them move forward?

This is one of the key areas for motivational work. If you already a coach you will know all about this, but if not, it is another string that you can add to your bow. Not only does it improve the outcome for your client, but it makes them feel better about you, and so are likely to recommend you more, and also your market expands to include those who "don't need therapy".

Incidentally, clients who come to you to resolve problems may be reluctant to talk about you to their friends and colleagues:

some feel that seeking help is a weakness. However, if they see you as being akin to a "personal trainer for the mind", they are much more likely to talk about it: in fact having a coach can be perceived as a status symbol and demonstrates a person's commitment to progress.

Fear

Whatever sort of therapeutic work you are involved in, fear will play its part. Whether clients approach you to help them overcome their fear, or whether it is simply a background issue, it will be relevant. Maybe you also find that clients can be afraid of you and your therapy!

It can be useful to point out to a client the difference between fear and respect. Here are some examples:

- It may be inappropriate to have a phobia of snakes, but if approached by a cobra, it is a good thing to respect it and the harm it can do.
- You may "know" that you have no need to fear taking an exam, but "knowing" doesn't stop the feeling. Changing the perspective to respect for the process and the importance of the outcome can make all the difference.
- I heard a boxer say that he did not fear his opponent, he respected him. Which attitude is likely to produce the best result?
- A client once said that they had an overriding fear of ill-health. This soon turned round to him having a huge respect for his body and his good health.

Fear and regret

"Fear is temporary- regret is permanent"

This anonymous quote was provided by Steve Wilson. He has found it useful when working with clients who are afraid.

Commitment

As therapists or coaches it is imperative that we are committed to our clients. Our clients' needs are paramount and if we forget this and deliver a sub-standard service, nobody will benefit. This probably sounds quite tautological so far, but what does being committed to our clients mean in practice?

If you have trained in one modality, you may well be clear as to what you are committed to, but modalities vary. For example, when I (Fiona) trained as a counsellor, much emphasis was put on "not getting hung up on results". The basis for this is that the client is responsible for their progress and that the counsellor is not there to "fix it". If however you are a coach, you will probably be horrified at this attitude as in coaching, getting results is what it is all about.

These angles are not immediately easy to reconcile, until I realised that these modalities have a significant factor in common. That is autonomy of the client. Even within the coaching relationship, accountability to the coach is created in order to assist the client to achieve what they wish to achieve. Responsibility for success still remains with the client. Perhaps the key difference between the modalities is what you, as the coach/counsellor, do with your commitment to the process.

Here is a list of factors that I believe are crucial to having, and demonstrating commitment to the client in whatever modality:

- time integrity
- being 99% WITH the client when you are with them, or talking on the phone, emailing etc. (I say 99% because I do not believe 100% is achievable)
- ensuring that as much as possible is done to ensure that nothing and no one disturbs you when you are with the client
- behaving appropriately and respectfully during your time with the client
- adhering to codes of ethics
- valuing the client's model of the world

- being happy to accept that responsibility for the results of the process are essentially your clients
- being willing to do whatever is required (within the remit of your modality) to ensure that you assist the client to meet their goals, or not as THEY choose
- being prepared to put in whatever effort is required between sessions to ensure good practice

What does commitment mean to you?

Anger

For every minute you are angry, you lose sixty seconds of happiness.
Ralph Waldo Emerson

Anger is an emotion that many therapists find difficult to work with. It can also be difficult to experience! Looking at the above quote, it seems to be saying that anger is a negative thing. But is it? Maybe a minute of anger can be more useful than 60 seconds of happiness, if it is appropriate. Maybe a minute of anger can lead to lots more happiness in the future. It's all a question of balance.

Experienced therapists will tell you that clients vary incredibly on this score, and that anger is a complex issue. How can you assist a client to have an appropriate level of anger in their lives? Maybe these considerations can help:

- avoiding judging your client for their anger or lack of it
- avoiding colluding with your client. An example of collusion would be saying "you have every right to be angry". Perhaps they do, but this is their choice, not yours!
- accepting their anger or lack of it
- being willing to listen to expressions of anger, however inappropriate they, or you, feel they are
- recognising that anger is often a choice and that as such there are no right or wrong choices
- recognising that anger can be harmful at either end of the continuum (ie too little or too much)

97

Anger (2)

"Holding anger is like grasping a hot coal with the intent of throwing it at someone else; you are the one who gets burned."

The Buddha

Anger is sometimes appropriate and as many clients (perhaps more) have a problem with allowing anger as those who have too much. But this quote clearly demonstrates the need for anger to be let go. I have used this quote directly with clients to help them understand what they are doing to themselves by not dealing with this emotion.

Growing

You have to do your own growing no matter how tall your grandfather was.

Abraham Lincoln

An interesting thought! Obvious maybe, but as I read this quote I thought how useful it could be to share with clients who have still strong but limiting attachments to parental figures (adult clients of course!). I guess that Lincoln was referring to people who had "tall grandfathers", ie a background of status but perhaps this also applies to clients with "small" backgrounds and who maybe feel that they cannot grow beyond these boundaries.

Suggestibility

From Wayne Clayton-Robb

<u>"What is suggestibility?"</u>

Dr Yapko has given us a useful working definition of 'suggestibility'. He posits that:

'It is an openness to accepting and responding to new ideas, new information.'[1]

In our day to day lives, our potential for suggestibility is laid siege to by our families, our employers and the media in particular and many other disparate bodies and organisations in general. They assail us with communications which are generally couched to influence our thoughts and/or promote a course of action i.e. to accept a political viewpoint or purchase a particular product, be it that pair of 'Nike' trainers that no child can be seen without or the fact that I can have any 4 books of my choice, from the genre of my choice for 99p, If I join a particular book club.

Successful selling, whether it is of ideology or merchandise, demands a powerful communication that absorbs a person's full attention, particularly at an emotional level. Thus as Paul Watzlawack has pointed out aspects of any piece of communication and ergo advertising 'can have hypnotic (i.e., absorbing and influential qualities without formally being "hypnosis" (Watzlawack 1985)'

On a warm, summer's day when my 11 year old daughter's senses have been alerted by the sound of the ice –cream van's chimes, she generates feelings and recognitions associated with a large, smooth, whipped ice –cream cone, harbouring a chocolate flake. Her demands to be united with said ice –cream are a direct response to the sounds generated by the van, the messages painted on its side and the images of various mouth-watering ice-cream concoctions bedecking the serving hatch. What clearly happens here is that her critical facultes have been temporarily bypassed by an effective appeal to her sensory perceptions and will only resume normal service when she is asked to tidy her room. Of course, as an effective communicator, one is able to give her what Erickson called the 'Illusion of Choice', when I ask her if she would like to tidy her room up first or do her homework.

Therefore, the effective advertiser is also an effective communicator, who uses a wide-range of devices, including: words, sounds, images and colours to circumvent the critical faculty of our mind and appeal directly to our feelings, memories and values in an attempt to influence the way we buy, vote etc.

It follows then, that in order to help our clients bring about the effective changes that they are hoping to make, we to must be or become effective communicators. Additionally, the development of the client/therapist relationship through rapport building, empathy and establishing client expectation is vital to the achievement of a successful outcome.

It is often from the everyday hypnosis that we draw our confidence building examples. One that I frequently use In explaining the power of the unconscious mind is the fact that our conscious mind can only deal with 7+ or – 2 pieces of information at any one time. Isn't it wonderful then, that we have an unconscious mind that enables us to carry out a wide-range of driving functions whilst listening to the stereo, and talking to the wife and children at the same time? Isn't it strange when you suddenly find yourself 20 miles further up the motorway? Everything is fine though, your unconscious mind was in control all of the time and had some unusual or emergency situation occurred it would have let you know. Isn't that awesome? Hopefully, in this instance, I have achieved several things. I have created a powerful mental expectancy within the client. I have helped build rapport by reference to everyday hypnosis and as a bonus; I may well have a 'Yes Set'

So it can be seen, that there is much common ground between everyday suggestibility and the clinical experience. Both are referencing the 'creative flux' of the unconscious mind with a view to guiding the recipient's choices whether to purchase a certain brand of toothpaste or to the possibilities of making life-affirming changes.

REFERENCES

1. Yapko Michael D (1995) Essentials of Hypnosis Bruner/Mazel New York

SELECT BIBLIOGRAPHY

1. Waxman David (1989) Hartland's Medical and Dental Hypnosis Third Edition. Bailliere Tindall London
2. Sommer Carol (1992) Conversational Hypnosis. Sommer, Illinois

Forgiveness

When we are doing therapy with our clients, do we need to consider the need for forgiveness? With religion being less and less important in western society, the idea of being able to see someone of prestige who has the "authority" to forgive people of their "sins" is falling to increasingly to the therapist. In my own practice, I often give the client the suggestion that it has come time for them to forgive themselves for whatever they have done in order for the client to move forward. I am not doing the forgiving, but rather facilitating their own forgiveness of themselves. Never underestimate the power of forgiveness, which can often move our clients further and faster than with traditional therapeutic interventions.

Self-image

Iris Murdoch once said *"the chief requirement of the good life.... is to live without any image of oneself.... what we need most is precisely to see reality.... outside us"*.

How can one live without ANY image of oneself? This quote was given at a talk from a psycho-analyst who insisted that this sentiment is true, and attempted to link it to self-centredness, but this is an entirely different issue. It did, however, make me think about what a "healthy" self-image "should" be. As therapists we are constantly working with people who have self-image problems. Maybe every client is working on self-image fundamentally. Even a smoker who is wanting to quit is working on changing his self-image to that of a non-smoker.

I have looked back over the clients I have seen during the last fortnight, and I can see that for every one of them, there was

101

(or is) a confusion over self-image. Confusion as to ability to be who they choose to be, confusion as to what they ARE, and sometimes confusion as to the difference in the image they have of themselves and the images that others have of them.

So, maybe resolving this confusion is a key to successful therapy. Those of you who are familiar with logical levels will no doubt see this as at least an overlap with the identity level. Something to explore some more perhaps.

Contracts in therapy

Earlier in this chapter (p91), James Malone contributed an article which included the line: *"One hypnotherapist I know of here in New Jersey who is also a lawyer actually made official looking contracts for his clients to sign"*. This prompted some interest from those who regularly use contracts, so we asked Martin Armstrong Prior (who has a special interest in this area) to write for us. Here is his piece:

In essence all therapy is done as a consequence of an agreement or contract. The contract may be verbal or written.

Contracts are normally the result of an offer and an acceptance of terms. These terms may relate to general rules or conditions under which therapy is carried out or the may relate to detail of techniques or procedures to be used. The construction of detailed contracts for each individual's therapy is a time consuming and complex procedure and is arguably unnecessary. A much simpler and more easily explained form is the general version that implies a link to another document containing diagnostic and technical details, i.e. a Client/Patient Notation and File. This is frequently referred to as "the Case Notes".

So leaving the detail of the diagnosis and the strategy for treatment to the case notes Contracts can be seen simply as a framework within which Therapy is conducted. There are many possibilities for the format of such a contract. There are a few basic rules:

- *Own the document – you are offering it so use your headed paper,*
- *Clearly identify the parties to the agreement – you as therapist and the name of the client/patient,*
- *State the cost of the sessions and the terms under which costs can be varied,*
- *Include a session cancellation clause – then they can't complain if the bailiff calls,*
- *Make it clear how the parties will communicate and include a 'harassment' clause,*
- *Give their right to access the Complaints Procedure – don't be afraid, this will not increase the likelihood of you getting complaints quite the reverse, as with other double binds the effect is positive!*
- *State how you record sessions, if you use audio of video recording – I have never had anyone ask for it to be turned off IN TWELVE YEARS!*
- *Finally help them to feel in control by including a renegotiation clause – this can be very useful as it means you can keep working while you sort out changes of direction, mode of therapy or costs, etc. They also feel more in control and less controlled by you.*

What advantages does all this work bring?

- *Professionalism – they feel they are dealing with the real article,*
- *Security - for both parties to the contract,*
- *Clarity - simple wording removes confusion and supports rapport,*
- *Safety – they cannot say they did not know if they have a copy of the contract! It makes dealing with a complaint simpler, should one arise.*

What are the disadvantages?

- *One more form – just one, keep a photocopy on file and give them the original,*

- *You need to explain it to them – talking it through improves rapport,*
- *Sorry I can't think of any more.*

Remember – don't be afraid of contracts. They are there to help you and have certainly helped me. I'm sure they have reduced the numbers of time wasters and failures to attend appointments. So far from costing me they have helped me earn more.

Letting go

There's an important difference between giving up and letting go.
Jessica Hatchigan

I expect you would agree that many if not most of our clients have problems with letting go. Letting go of emotions, the past, relationships. This can take many forms, but not letting go, when appropriate can hold us back. I wonder though, how often clients may feel that letting go, means giving up? Obviously this will depend on the type of letting go. For example if a client needs to let go of emotion surrounding an accident in childhood, this is not likely to link into a feeling of failure, but it might if the same person was looking at letting go of a relationship that she "ought" to have made work.

There is also the interpretation of "giving up" in terms of losing out. If a person gives up smoking, they may feel that they are losing out, but by letting go of the habit, they may feel more positive and recognise that they are simply adapting to more appropriate behaviours.

Chocolate

Strength is the capacity to break a chocolate bar into four pieces with your bare hands--and then just eat one of the pieces.
Judith Viorst

At the time of writing, this week of the year is maybe the key week for thinking about the whole issue of eating, dieting, exercise and weight control. Why? We've just had Easter, with the prevalence of chocolate, and now we are moving towards summer, which means (in the UK!), better weather, longer days, and skimpier clothes.

Therefore there is possibly much more motivation for getting fit and shedding pounds. So, where does chocolate come into the equation? Chocolate can be considered to represent the whole weight control problem:

- it is pleasurable for most people to eat chocolate
- chocolate not only tastes nice, but makes a chemical difference
- eating chocolate is often associated with being treated, loved, comforted
- chocolate contains processed sugar: according to Gerald Kein's article in the Journal of Hypnotism, this is a poison and we should not eat it at all!
- chocolate is high fat
- chocolate is also linked to inactivity for many. How does the idea of flopping on the sofa with a bar of chocolate make you feel?

So, what can we do about all this? We need to (for ourselves and clients), ensure that we do not feel punished, that we get our needs for love and relaxation met, and that whatever we do, we feel good about it and about ourselves.

As indicated in the quote above, the key is CONTROL. Gerry Kein may be technically correct, but I believe that true control is when you can have a little bit of chocolate (or whatever) now and again and when you do, you are choosing to (not just eating it because it's there for example), and you ENJOY it.

This control is possible, if we change our pain/pleasure links. We can change the previous statements to

- it is pleasurable to NOT eat chocolate

- there are better ways to produce endorphins, such as walking in the sun
- I can feel loved, treated and comforted much more appropriately and truly
- my body deserves to be fed foods that help it, rather than ones it has to fight
- low fat foods lead to a low fat me
- if I lead an active and productive life, I can flop all I like without any guilt

Chocolate (2)

All I really need is love, but a little chocolate now and then doesn't hurt!

Lucy, Peanuts

For those of you who work with weight control, this quote may bring a wry smile. I have included it here though as it reminded me of a spate of chocolate advertising in the UK that is directed specifically at the link between chocolate and comfort eating. There are two products (which shall remain nameless) which have used this tactic. One even says something along the lines of "give in to your inner child". Am I alone in thinking this unethical?

Using your voice

As therapists, of whatever persuasion, we need to convey messages to our clients. Many of you are hypnotherapists, but this applies also to counsellors and psychotherapists. Of course the words we choose to use are crucial, but so is tone, and intent.

I heard an idea that can help to convey a message more accurately. This idea is to mentally "attach" a colour or texture (or both) to your words. We see this in print often: we are well aware of the difference that fonts and colours can make in advertising, so why not use this when we are talking.

I suggest you practice this. Take some standard phrases that you might use in a therapy session, and say them in blue, red, yellow, purple, black and green. How do they feel? Does one colour convey what you are intending better than another?

Try textures too. You may like to say a phrase smoothly, silkily, bumpily or roughly. How does this affect the message?

Respect

I (Shaun) was reminded today of a fellow student who I trained with long ago. Our training included a module on communication, and as part of this, we were encouraged to acknowledge our right to express ourselves, and to communicate our feelings and needs in ANY situation with ANY person.

However, what this chap (we will call him Chris) missed, was that our right to do so, also must incorporate the right of the other individual to be treated with respect. I witnessed three incidents where the fact that this was missed was demonstrated.

The first was in class, where he told another student that her contribution to the discussion was boring and that she should be quiet. He was, of course, entitled to have this opinion, but the other student was also entitled to say her bit. If Chris had incorporated respect, he would have been able, perhaps, to encourage her to find a way to be more succinct in future, thus getting both their needs met.

The second occasion was at a pub, when he verbally laid into the husband of a friend because this guy had lit a cigarette, before Chris had arrived. Again, if he had used some respect, Chris would have simply asked if it may be possible for him to refrain, now that he was here as he found the smoke a problem. The smoker then would have had a choice as to how to react.

The third occasion was when a visiting tutor attended the course, and Chris asked him why he thought that he had anything to teach us, as his branch of therapy was bunkum. A more respectful question might have been to ask whether he would be providing an explanation of why the tutor felt his therapy to be useful to us.

The reason that we write about this here, as we believe that respect is such a valuable component of what you can offer your clients. It detracts from nothing and adds so much!

By the way, Chris did get it in the end!

Coping with traumatic material

I don't know about you, but I was completely unprepared for the stories my clients would tell me following my basic hypnotherapy training. Luckily, I seemed to have a natural ability to listen, but not absorb, and this skill has been honed in other training. However, there are still times, even after 11 years, when it is not so easy to cope. Only this week, I was shocked by a client's history: I had thought I had heard it all! It was a very upsetting story, and I found it difficult to put to one side.

This issue is one that crops up regularly in our training courses, and in supervision. It is a critical skill to develop, and one key is to ensure that you always have somewhere to "dump" your feelings. This would usually be either supervision, or your own therapy, depending on how you have been affected. In the case described above I was immediately on the phone to my supervisor so that I could unload, express my distress, and move on. If however the content had stirred my own process, then I would have taken it to therapy, and worked on my issues there.

Writing can also help. When something is in writing, it need not be in your head. Also ensure that your boundaries are strong. This can include, among other things, setting fixed times for working, leaving all thoughts of clients in the office when you leave, or even something as simple as anchoring your work role to wearing certain clothes or shoes!

Self-views and estimates of performance

Let's have a look at the place in therapy of the development of belief in ability. Research has shown that views on ability are not greatly associated with actual ability. We all have seen clients who diminish their own sense of achievement, but also there are those who over-estimate. This leads us to think that our role as therapists is to encourage clients to have a greater awareness of the real situation, bearing in mind that all is subjective, and then to a greater awareness of possibilities.

We like to use the motto, "If others can, I can", but this needs also the recognition that even if "I can", this doesn't necessarily mean that I can do it without training and practice, nor that I can necessarily do it as well as others.

Choice

From James Malone:

How many people are trapped in their everyday habits: part numb, part frightened, part indifferent? To have a better life we must keep choosing how we're living.

Albert Einstein

Would you agree that one of most critical factors in any therapy is helping the client to recognise their choices, and the resources that they have, or can develop, to enable them to action their choices?

Choice (2)

From Jane Watson:

On the subject of choices... *I believe that clients are very often clients precisely because they have unwittingly chosen to alter situations and other people, instead of correctly choosing to alter behavioural responses (or situational factors) that they actually have the power to change.*

109

H A L T! – standing for

*HUNGRY, ANGRY, LONELY & TIRED is commonly used in addiction counselling to make clients aware of potential triggers to binge-type behaviours. To these can be added specific situations and moods suggested by the client, including boredom, depression and anxiety. All can trigger episodes of self-harming behaviours that lead to further negative self-evaluation, escalate mood disorders and intensify feelings of being out of control. Loss of control in only one area of our lives can provoke panic and desperation but, fortunately, the reverse is also true; gaining control of apparently secondary symptoms can restore a sense of mastery and self-determination. Many clients with habit disorders present with chaotic eating or drinking patterns, and depression is frequently marked by weight gain or loss. Low and erratically fluctuating blood sugar levels have been shown to aggravate negative mood states. **Distressed clients sometimes seem intent on controlling things that are outside their sphere of influence – if we can help them focus on things they can control (including their own behaviours) they will hopefully find themselves on the road to recovery.***

Conscious/unconscious integration

On the Saturday afternoon of the 2004 NCH conference we were treated to a "once only" special: Shaun Brookhouse and Trevor Silvester, together, nothing prepared, just answering questions from the audience. Not only was this exceedingly entertaining (validating the Eric and Ernie title Shaun had awarded them), but educational and inspiring too.

One demonstration involved a member of the audience who wanted to develop enthusiasm for working with smoking cessation. Shaun and Trevor instinctively worked together, with Shaun addressing the unconscious (via whispered positive suggestions into the right ear), while Trevor maintained a conscious dialogue analysing the issue.

Looking backwards

"The farther backward you can look, the farther forward you are likely to see."

Winston Churchill

Churchill was talking (I believe) about understanding of history and how this affects a person's ability to understand possible future scenarios. Perhaps in the therapeutic field we can see this not only in terms of history of the world, but also of the individual. Not only the individual's life, but their family history can be included in this process.

Habits

"Habit is stronger than reason."

George Santayana

Whatever therapeutic role you have, you will be working with people with habits. We all have them, even if they are not obvious. Recognising that reason has little impact on a habit can be a useful place to start!

Aims

At Solid Gold in Las Vegas 2004, Ormond McGill suggested that therapists get their clients to write down what they want in one sentence. Obviously this may be over-simplistic in some circumstances, but it can really help to get the client focused and to ensure that the therapist fully understands the client's aim.

His technique was to give the client a blank A4 sheet at the start of each session, on which they were encouraged to write their sentence. This can also help a client to be aware of progress that they are making.

Computing metaphor

This idea is one only to be used with clients who will know what you are talking about! The idea is to liken the process of therapy with the Scandisk program, ie, that therapy can search through your mental hard drive, find work with them. If Scandisk finds an error, it gives options to delete a file, fix the file or ignore. We can do just the same with emotional issues. Scandisk also allows for a backup to be taken in case the process makes things worse. Once again, we can do that, and we can also replicate the process of marking an area as a problem. For example, recognising that a certain experience was terrible, but leaving the memory as is, and just taking the learning forward, leaving emotion behind.

A tale from the front

From Mureen Hunt:

Trust in the force.

Think of Vera in Giles and you've got the client I spent eight sessions with; the last two being a couple of weeks apart for her to experience, in trance, a really good communion before the actual event.

Skip forwards four months and she has returned to full time teaching with a new class who are little horrors, and the return of her symptoms. Her face had lost the drawn haunted expression, but she described, 'it' as 'taking her over' and her hands moved over the left side of her head and body. She is left handed.

I recognise that I had options that I didn't use and some which I'm not trained to use.

At the NCH Conference I gained some skills which I have used successfully. We agreed to use these skills.

She claimed a SUD of 8 and we started with the Breath

Optimised Trauma Unblocking (BOTAU) and the SUD was reduced to 7, 7/6, 6. Since the client doesn't know that this was supposed to work like magic - alone - I followed this with the finger following demonstrated by Mark, this produced a SUD of 6, BOTAU 6, finger following 6, Swish 6, and for good measure the stage 3 of the BOTAU, the unblocking, which left us with a SUD of, you've guessed it - 6!

Recognising, by this time, that something else was needed we did a lovely induction that encompassed all our previous work and followed this with a slightly spiritual experience of (forgiveness) letting go of the past, complete with an owl as the power animal.

I would not accept a further appointment and said that if one was needed then we were dealing with a different issue to the one previously worked through.

I received a little card expressing that she had enjoyed the silver wedding party she had attended.

Whew.

What other people think

We probably wouldn't worry about what people think of us if we could know how seldom they do.

Olin Miller

Isn't this one of the major issues that clients have? Usually not the issue they raise initially, but so often a factor underlying other issues. Think of the most typical problems that hypnotherapists work with, smoking, weight control, anxiety, stress. All of these are likely to have this element. So what do we do about it? Do we need to work with it at all; surely it is normal to care how others see you?

The answer depends on the client. Just keep it in mind!

Vulnerability

I (Fiona) was talking with a supervisee and we discussed the issue of vulnerability. Is everyone vulnerable? I said that I believed so, but he claimed not. Perhaps the answer is in degree, and the critical factor that vulnerability does not always show from the outside. Just because someone does not appear vulnerable does that mean they are not? Many are so adept at creating an image and keeping their feelings in, in order to keep themselves safe that it may well be that the one person who you perceive as being tough as old boots is actually as vulnerable as most on the inside.

So what is the lesson here? I would say that it is to presume vulnerability always. It gives your client permission to express themselves, and what is more important than that. Also, it is crucial that you are clear in your communications. Vulnerable people (or all of us) may be prone to interpret anything that you say in the negative if you lack clarity.

Who not to work with

Our readership covers a huge range of therapies, but the largest single group is of hypnotherapists. We have been asked to write about contraindications for working with hypnosis by a UK trainer, so please forgive us for writing specifically for hypnotherapists at this time.

There are various categories of clients who we should not work with:

1.   those who are beyond our capacity to help. This group would include people who are mentally ill (eg schizophrenic or psychotic), or those who are not considered to be hypnotizable (eg the very young, very low IQ, or someone drunk/drugged)
2.   those who we are not trained to work with. Specific training is required for working with children, eating disorders, depression, to name just a few.
3.   those with medical conditions that may be contra-indicated. Let's look at some specifics. Diabetes: you

can work with diabetics, but you need to ensure that they are fully in balance at the start of each session. Epilepsy: only work with this under medical referral, and if their epilepsy is controlled by medication. Do not use eye fixation inductions. Asthma: you can work with asthmatics, but ensure that they have their inhaler to hand and that they are aware that there is a possibility of needing it.

4. those who have issues that you have issue with. If a client or their issues "press your buttons", refer them on. This is in their best interests and yours. It is a sign of your strength that you can recognize times when you cannot work with someone.

Addressing clients

An Inspirations reader emailed to ask our opinion of a fellow therapist who, allegedly, called a female enquirer "my poppet" throughout the phone call. In our opinion this is an unprofessional approach which is damaging to all of us. We all need to take great care in our use of language with all clients, and be aware that use of certain phrases and nomenclature may be offensive to some. It is easiest to use the benchmark of what you would expect if you visited another professional (eg doctor, dentist, accountant, lawyer). I know that I would simply expect to be called Fiona, or perhaps Mrs Biddle (whereupon I would say, please call me Fiona). I live in the East Midlands; if I am in a shop, it is normal to be addressed as "love" or "duck" (for our non-UK readers these names may seem weird, I know!) This is what is expected, so it is fine. But if a professional called me either of those, it would jar. Certainly if anyone I was not exceptionally close to called me "my poppet", any rapport would be damaged irrevocably!

Boundaries

Please note, the following is based on practice and law in the UK: other countries may be different.

We have been asked to comment on where the boundary should fall between client and therapist, particularly with regard to friendship and dating. It is possible to draw the line in several places, but the codes of ethics the authors subscribe to are quite clear. This is that if any relationship other than a therapeutic one should develop, therapy must be terminated as soon as possible. This includes business or sexual relationship and we would interpret this as meaning friendships as in, say, going to the pub together, but of course we can be "friendly" with our clients.

So, to summarise: It is unethical to take as a client anyone with whom you have another relationship, and it is unethical to continue therapy with anyone with whom another relationship begins. A specific part of the question was whether any particular amount of time should elapse after therapy is concluded before a therapist may date a client. The answer is no. This is not written in stone (in our codes, but please do check your own!). However, if a relationship were to go wrong any hint that the therapist was using their influence to persuade a client to date them would be very seriously frowned upon, so take extreme care.

It is best to consider there to be three sexes in the world: male, female and client (the latter also includes students and supervisees!). Stick with your usual sexual preference and leave the latter category out of the equation!

A case study

From Tom Robertson:

Talking to Dolphins
(Weaving a Treatment Strategy into a Child's Fantasies}

This brief article describes one example of how a treatment strategy was successfully interwoven into a child's fantasy, to bring about a major improvement. Because children have such vivid imaginations and few inhibitions, I believe the technique can be used to treat many of their problems and conditions.

Susie was 8 years old when her parents first brought her to me. She had been suffering from terrible bouts of severe tummy pain and cramps for many weeks. Her pallor was pale, she was not eating well and her fragile appearance indicated her suffering. Medical diagnosis ranged from an ongoing tummy bug to irritable bowel syndrome. She was treated with a range of medicines from Calpol, antacids to antispasmodics, with little relief. Sometimes heat from a hot water bottle would ease the pain a bit.

Her mother indicated that Susie was very sensitive and worried a lot, about many things. However, she was reluctant to discuss her worries with her mother or anyone. As conventional medicine practice was not helping Susie, her mother considered hypnotherapy as an alternative approach, after discussing the situation with me. I asked her to seek her GP's approval, which was willingly given.

During the all important first session (and essentially, communicating at the child's level), Susie revealed that she loved animals, especially dolphins and would imagine swimming with them. Capitalising on the revelation, I asked her to close her eyes and imagine that she was now swimming with them. She did this with ease, describing two dolphins, one of which was her close friend. I asked her to tell her 'friend' about all of her worries and that perhaps she would like to tell me too, as I also loved dolphins.

When she opened her eyes, she did tell me about a number of her worries. In particular, she was scared of her school teacher feeling that she was always being singled out and shouted at. Another major concern centred on relationships with her classmates - one with whom she had a quarrel, was trying to steal her best friend. Finally, before commencing hypnosis, I asked her to draw her tummy and show me where the pain affected her.

Secondary gain was clear; her tummy spasms meant she spent a lot of time away from school.

I decided to capitalise on her vivid portrayal of swimming with the dolphins to develop and implement a treatment strategy to manage her pain and relieve her worries.

I gave her a 'magic' coin to focus her gaze and then put her into a relatively deep trance. I suggested that she was swimming in warm water with her dolphin friend and its companion. She responded positively. I had her tell all of her worries to her dolphin friend, who then passed them to its companion to flick away with its nose. Once flicked away, she would feel happy and carefree. I next suggested that the heat from the warm water would sooth her tummy pain. I had the dolphins take her to a nearby bay to drink a special blackcurrant flavoured drink (her choice of flavour!) that would eliminate the pain, totally. While drinking it, I had her imagine the liquid going down into the painful area of her tummy, (based on her drawing) and starting to heal it. Finally, she was taught under hypnosis to use the magic coin to hypnotise herself and to use the dolphin scenarios to help her whenever she encountered pain or stress. A tape recording was made for her use, too.

On returning for the second session, she had improved considerably and was able to reduce her pain using the techniques taught to her. In addition she had named her dolphins as 'Sparky' and 'Flick' which heightened the impact of the dolphin scenario. I was able to create a number of additional scenarios around Sparky and Flick, which, for example, helped her to change her perception of the teacher and classmates.

From the third session onwards, her pain and worries had totally gone. Life is now normal for her and she enjoys school, at last!

Recording sessions

We used not to record sessions but now do so routinely. This follows a spurious, but very serious allegation of impropriety that showed the need for protection of the therapist from potential damage from a client. We strongly suggest that if you do not already do so, that audio recording becomes a routine part of your practice. Clients are informed via the disclosure statement at the start of therapy, and no one objects.

It is easy to do this nowadays using the latest recorders which can download to CD via a USB port. I (Shaun) can fit a whole weeks sessions on one CD; and I see up to 45 clients in that time!

Starting over

Though no one can go back and make a brand new start, anyone can start from now and make a brand new ending.

Carl Bard

How often is this an idea that can help your clients? I have printed this up on business cards printed from my computer, and give a copy to clients (when appropriate) to remind them that the past is the past, but the future is theirs to design.

What do clients want out of life?

A perfect summer day is when the sun is shining, the breeze is blowing, the birds are singing, and the lawn mower is broken.

James Dent

This quote made me wonder about what people really want. Isn't the work/leisure balance absolutely critical? How often is this at the root of dissatisfaction, or at least a contributory cause? And, of course the "right" balance is something only the individual can determine.

Choice

"You always do what you want to do. This is true with every act. You may say that you had to do something, or that you were forced to, but actually, whatever you do, you do by choice. Only you have the power to choose for yourself."

W Clement Stone

One of the hardest lessons that we need to teach our clients.... And ourselves?

Pain and change

When the pain of staying the same is greater than pain of changing, you have the right environment for change. Also, the pain of staying the same can be maximised, and of changing, minimised.

Carrying the client's burden

I heard what I see as a lovely, if partial, definition of therapy: to carry the client's burden for the time they are with you. Isn't this important? The client is likely to be carrying their problem around with them all the time, but when they are with you, you are at least sharing the burden with them, helping them to examine what it really is, and to explore how, and indeed whether, it could be put down permanently. It's thoughts like this that remind me of what a wonderful service we offer!

Advice

Advice is what we ask for when we already know the answer but wish we didn't.

Erica Jong

Remember this when your clients attempt to coerce you into giving advice! Just think of the trouble you could get into if a) you tell them the answer they already know which they do not want to hear, or b) if you tell them something different!

If you are a coach, when advice is appropriate, also beware and preframe your suggestions appropriately.

Transformation

The meeting of two personalities is like the contact of two chemical substances: if there is any reaction, both are transformed.

Carl Jung (1875 - 1961)

This is an interesting point. If you do your job correctly and create this "reaction", you can expect to be transformed too!

Struggle

From John Lawrence:

*I came across a story titled **The Butterfly** (author unknown) that reflects on this point:*
A man found a cocoon of a butterfly. One day a small opening appeared. He sat and watched the butterfly for several hours as it struggled to force its body through that little hole.

Then it seemed to stop making any progress. It appeared as if it had gotten as far as it could, and it could go no further.

So the man decided to help the butterfly. He took a pair of scissors and snipped off the remaining bit of the cocoon.

The butterfly then emerged easily. But it had a swollen body and small, shriveled wings. The man continued to watch the butterfly because he expected that, at any moment, the wings would enlarge and expand to be able to support the body, which would contract in time.

Neither happened! In fact, the butterfly spent the rest of its life crawling around with a swollen body and shriveled wings.

It never was able to fly.

What the man, in his kindness and haste, didn't understand was that the restricting cocoon and the struggle required for the butterfly to get through the tiny opening were Nature's way of forcing fluid from the body of the butterfly into its wings so that it would be ready for flight once it achieved its freedom from the cocoon.

Sometimes struggles are exactly what we need in our lives.

If we were allowed to go through life without any obstacles we would be crippled. We would not be as strong as what we could have been. We would never fly!

Meditation

Half an hour's meditation each day is essential, except when you are busy. Then a full hour is needed.

St. Francis de Sales

Many readers of Inspirations are hypnotherapists and they will all know how beneficial clients find the process of relaxation in their consulting room. But is this something that you actually suggest that they continue? Self-hypnosis is such an effective tool to teach to our clients (or meditation, or simply relaxation with a purpose). Are you, and consequently your clients, missing out?

Having a right

To have a right to do a thing is not at all the same as to be right in doing it.

G.K. Chesterton

In today's world of "human rights" this can often be forgotten. A client today mentioned that he felt unable to tell an employee that their work was poor due to political correctness. An interesting situation and one that we can all recognize. The employee has a right to be treated with respect, and I think we can agree that my client is right to do so. But my client also has a right to ensure that she does her job, and is right to do so (that is his job). He may even have a right to be angry with her (don't we all have a right to be angry?), but it is not right for him to express this as this interferes with her right to be safe (maybe...). And what about her right to be angry with him if he doesn't guide her properly? Complicated isn't it?

Working with big dreams

"Dream big, not small. Small dreams are not worth getting out of bed for"

Anon

To start with, let's look at what we mean by big dreams. They will vary in "big-ness" from person to person. One client may think that being a millionaire this time next year is quite reasonable and to them the big dream would be being a billionaire. Conversely, I once had a client whose big dream was to become a brick layer. The common denominator is the fact that the client doesn't really believe it to be possible. We are looking for the impossible. Typically the client will say that their dream would be good but it is "ridiculous".

Why then look for the big dream? The answer is that by doing so, the client is likely to strive further than they would if they just looked for their SMART goal (SMART being specific, measurable, attainable (or adjustable), realistic and time-oriented).

For example, a therapist may set themselves a SMART goal of seeing 10 clients a week in six months time. However, if encouraged to examine their big dreams they may find that they want 30 clients a week and to be training. This may seem impossible (or ridiculous) at the time, but by imagining this they may get to their 10 a week more quickly, and start to move towards a belief that the rest, just maybe, could, one day, be possible.

Maturity

Maturity is the ability to do a job whether or not you are supervised, to carry money without spending it, and to bear an injustice without wanting to get even.

Ann Landers

Of course this quote caught my eye because of the reference to supervision. It is an interesting thought. A mature therapist CAN do their job without supervision, but all the staff of the UK Academy agree that they will not do it as well as they would if they had supervision. Of course this quote is not about therapy per se, but it is important to recognize the benefit that we can ALL get from having a system of professional support!

What matters?

'The harder the conflict, the more glorious the triumph. What we obtain too cheap, we esteem too lightly; it is dearness only that gives everything its value. I love the man that can smile in trouble, that can gather strength from distress and grow brave by reflection. 'Tis the business of little minds to shrink; but he whose heart is firm, and whose conscience approves his conduct, will pursue his principles unto death."

Thomas Paine

Decathlons

Your life is more like a decathlon than a single event. Sometimes you have to work to be better at one event in order to be able to improve in another. Every event helps your total score.

Frank Dick

A useful metaphor when working with clients with life imbalance.

Champions League Final

This article was originally written following the match in May 2005. AC Milan scored within the first minute and were 3-0 up at half time. Liverpool then scored 3 goals within 7 minutes in the second half, and the game was decided on a penalty shoot out which Liverpool won. Why am I telling you this? Because it brought to mind the concept of belief and expectation.

I heard that the AC Milan coach had said that they would score within the first three minutes. Did this have an effect on the fact that they did? Did they score because they, and Liverpool, believed they would? Wouldn't it be interesting to know? And what about the Liverpool come back? How much of that was down to belief, on either side?

Of course, we just can't know the answers to these questions, but what we do know is that our clients' beliefs will affect their chances of achieving what they are in therapy to achieve. If they believe that all will be well, and if they believe that you can help them, so much the better. How can you influence their beliefs?

Backpack full of rocks

I heard this idea from Devin Hastings: he suggested that the mind can be seen as a backpack full of rocks to represent past pain that we carry around. But no one has told us we can put the bag down, or even empty it. You can be the one to "give permission" to your clients to do so.

Appropriate Responsibility

I wonder if you have ever noticed that clients sometimes have a tendency to take responsibility for things that they have no control over yet do not take responsibility for the things they do. A suggestion that one can give to clients, and to ourselves, is an adaptation of the prayer of St Francis, "I strive to know the difference between that which I can and that which I cannot change and act appropriately in both circumstances"

Panning for gold

This idea came from the presentation at the 2005 NCH Conference by Brian Roet. When we are going through life, we are very much like 1890's prospectors for gold; you have to sift through tons of mud very often to find that elusive nugget of gold. We as therapists assist our clients to sift more effectively in order for them to discover their piece of gold.

Fast phobia

The above technique is often associated with NLP, but the technique actually was first discussed in The Practical Applications of Medical and Dental Hypnosis by Milton H Erickson, Seymour Hershman and Irving Secter in 1961. We are often asked how one can make this technique more effective, we say do the process in trance and you will maximise your success.

The time machine

The following technique is a very nice regressive reframe for your clients:

You have now become <u>so</u> deeply relaxed...<u>so</u> deeply relaxed...that your mind has become <u>so</u> sensitive...<u>so</u> receptive to what I say...that <u>everything</u> that I put into your mind...will sink so deeply into the unconscious part of your mind...and will cause so deep and lasting an impression there...that <u>nothing</u> will eradicate it...Consequently...these things that I put into your unconscious mind...will begin to exercise a greater and greater influence over the way you think...over the way you feel...over the way you behave...

And...because these things <u>will</u> remain...firmly imbedded in the unconscious part of your mind...after you have left here...when you are no longer with me...they will continue to exercise that same great influence...over your <u>thoughts</u>...your <u>feelings</u>...and your <u>actions</u>...<u>just</u> as strongly...<u>just</u> as surely...<u>just</u> as powerfully...when you are back home...or at work...as when you are with me in this room...You are now so <u>very deeply relaxed</u>...that <u>everything</u> that I tell you that is going to happen to you...<u>for your own good</u>...<u>will</u> happen...<u>exactly</u> as I tell you...

And<u> every feeling</u>...that I tell you that you will experience...you <u>will</u> experience...<u>exactly</u> as I tell you...And these same things <u>will continue to happen</u> to you...<u>every day</u>...and<u> you will continue to experience </u>these same feelings...<u>every day</u>...<u>just</u> as strongly...<u>just</u> as surely...<u>just</u> as powerfully...when you are back home...or at work...as when you are with me in this room...

I would like you to use your active imagination and visualise a personal Time Machine. The machine is unique to you and has glass windows on all sides. I would like you to take a ride in this time machine, back to the time when this problem began.

When you get there you will be able to observe everything as an observer, you will not be in the situation that you go back to. When you get there let me know.

Now that you are there, notice what is happening, what is being said what you saw, and what was being felt. Notice, what is there for me to learn here. Once you get the necessary learning you can let go of the emotions attached to it, whilst retaining the learning. Notice also, when you get the learning, it effects your entire past present and future and the problem is reframed into something more appropriate for you.

5-PATH™
Here is a summary of 5-PATH, provided by its creator: © Calvin D. Banyan, The Hypnosis Center, Inc. All Rights Reserved.

5-PATH: The First Truly Powerful Systematic Approach to Hypnotherapy

History

After conducting research into hypnotherapeutic techniques, I was struck by the need to develop a systematic and virtually universal approach. I wanted to train the therapists at The Hypnosis Center, Inc, in a system that was relatively easy to learn, and easy to supervise. And, foremost, it had to be a system that provided good consistent results.
I was most impressed with the techniques that I learned from Gerald Kein at The Omni Hypnosis Training Center, in Deland, Florida.

Among the most important ideas and techniques that I learned were:

1. The need to properly prepare the client by sending a positive message, implying success from the very first contact, i.e., responding to questions about services with, "Yes, we do that all the time!"

2. The need to do a good pre-talk, where you focus on educating the client, and removing fears and misconceptions.
3. Using an appropriate hypnotic induction, usually a rapid or instant induction.
4. Utilizing a hidden test for somnambulism.
5. Using convincers, compounding of suggestions and direct drive techniques.
6. Using age regression to find the events that started the problem, using affect bridge.
7. Using informed child technique to change the effect (emotional or beliefs regarding incident).
8. Using the principle of forgiveness in therapy for others and the client.
9. Using Parts Therapy.
10. Using appropriate touch, to enhance the therapy.

These techniques and ideas were then organized into a systematic procedure that enhances each of the procedures as a whole, thus improving the outcome.

<u>Basically, Here Is How It Works</u>

The therapist will take the client through the following phases, each improving the success of the the subsequent phase (called a phase because more than one session may be necessary for procedure):

1. Direct Suggestion with Convincers
2. Age Regression and Informed Child Technique
3. Forgiveness of Others Therapy
4. Forgiveness of Self Therapy
5. Parts Mediation Therapy

How this is done is briefly outlined and explained below.

<u>Before the Hypnosis Session</u>

The therapist needs to be aware of the principles of waking suggestion, and how the client's degree of success is in part

128

determined by events that occur before the "hypnosis session" begins. The client's success is greatly increased if you are mindful of how the client is handled prior to the session. All of the following have an effect on the work you will be doing with the client.

1. Everything she has ever heard about hypnosis and you.
2. Your appearance and your office's appearance.
3. Any statements that you make about hypnosis or expected outcome.

Because of this you will need to make statements suggesting an expectation of a positive outcome. You and your office must be consistent with the message you intend to send (i.e., professional). You must do a good pre-hypnosis presentation, including a pre-talk and intake.

Then begins the five phases.

Phase I - Direct Suggestion

The focus of this phase of hypnosis is to have the client have a successful session. To accomplish this, the 5-PATH system consists of the following in Phase I:

1. Proper induction -- usually an instant or rapid induction.
2. Use of a hidden test for somnambulism.
3. Deepening.
4. Use of convincers--so that the client knows that she was hypnotized (i.e., eye lock).
5. Installation of suggestions for future success when doing hypnosis (i.e., post-hypnotic suggestion for rapid re-induction of hypnosis in future sessions).
6. Use of Direct Suggestion techniques, including giving some suggestions that were checked out with the client a head of time, in the pre-hypnosis interview (this puts the client at ease), giving suggestions appropriate to the issue, including the use of Compounding and Direct Drive techniques.

7. Making additional suggestions during the emerging process for post hypnotic suggestion (more convincers), such as time distortion and sensitivity to a color such as red.

Running a first session this way is done for the following reasons:

1. Using all of the above will improve the probability of a successful Direct Suggestion session.
2. Instill confidence in the client that she can use hypnosis for the issue she wants to work on.
3. Instill confidence in the client that she has selected a good hypnotherapist.
4. And, even more importantly perhaps, you have turned this person into an ideal client that will be great to work with in the future. This client, having gone through this procedure, will almost certainly experience a true Age Regression session (Phase II) with revivification.

Phase I, is done this way because it greatly increases the probability of success in Phase II, an Age Regression Session.

Phase II - Age Regression

Every problem that our clients come to see us about, have an origin, a beginning. The use of Age Regression Therapy is probably the most powerful tool available to a properly trained hypnotherapist. It is an essential part of 5-PATH. In addition to uncovering information from the past that might have become unavailable to the conscious mind, regression allows the therapist to "undo" the effects of the incident or incidents that have formed the problem. It is so important, that much of what was done in Phase I, was done so that we can have a successful Age Regression Session nearly every time.
It would go like this:

1. Use post-hypnotic suggestion for rapid re-induction of hypnosis to somnambulism.
2. Deepen.
3. Use Affect Bridge (usually).

130

4. Find ISE (initial sensitizing event).
5. Use Informed Child Technique.
6. Use Informed Adult Technique.
7. Progress into the future to experience success for the issue.
8. Use direct suggestion after change has been made.
9. Emerge, using suggestions for success.

The 5-PATH practitioner is encouraged to focus on the use of suggestion here. Remember that after you have accomplished Age Regression and Informed Child, the subconscious mind has been forced into a state of reorganization. Prior to this, the subconscious mind may have been resistant to suggestion, but now it is in a state of heightened suggestibility beyond what can be accomplished where Direct Suggestion techniques alone could accomplish.

Age Regression has now, increased our probability of success, even further because it has probably uncovered new information and provided additional insight, that both the client and therapist can use, as we continue into Phase III.

Phase III - Forgiveness of Others

The Age Regression session (Phase III) has provided us with great opportunities. The impact of the clients ISEs and SSE have been removed or reduced. You and the client have a much better understanding of the history of the problem/issue. And, most importantly to this phase, we know who the players are. We know about the people in our client's life that have been a part of the problem. In addition to gaining insight, and perhaps having been desensitized, the problem can be further healed by using forgiveness techniques. This provides for a reduction in emotion regarding the problem and a more complete releasing of the past, including the problem/issue.

It would go like this:

1. Do induction and deepening.

2. Set up for "Chair Therapy" where the client can confront or communicate with the person who was the contributor to the problem, i.e., abuser, parent, rapist, etc.
3. The situation is made so that the client will be completely safe in expressing her feelings (i.e., the offender cannot get out of a chair, etc.).
4. The client is encouraged to express how she feels or felt about what happened. The client is greatly encouraged to really let it all out.
5. Once the client is exhausted, the therapist has the client take the place of the offender, and will speak from that perspective.
6. Therapist then goes after the offender, similar to how the client did, but perhaps even stronger.
7. This will often cause new insight in the client with regard to the situation to occur which will be useful in accomplishing the forgiveness.
8. Dialog is encouraged between the client and the offender (the client will speak from both perspectives)
9. The client is then guided into forgiving the offender. It is explained to the client that this is for her own benefit and not for the benefit of the offender.
10. Then additional Direct Suggestion techniques are used, regarding the problem/issue.

This process of forgiveness may be repeated for additional players who contributed to the problem. And, the client may be encouraged to continue to forgive less significant persons on her own for a period during the session.

Notice the use of suggestion at the end of the process. Again, I want to remind the therapist that powerful techniques such as this force the subconscious mind into reorganization, and the client become exceptionally suggestible for suggestions that are consistent with the experience. Don't overlook this opportunity!

This phase again set us up for increased success in the following phase.

Phase IV - Self-Forgiveness

Most of my clients report that this phase of forgiving herself was the most important. I often wish that I could just go here first. But I believe that this phase is so successful because of the work done in the preceding phases.

It is essentially the same as Phase III, except this time the client take on two roles. The first role will be that of the "Self" and the other is the "Mistake-Making-Part." The Mistake-Making-Part, takes on the part of the offender in Phase III. This approach allows the client to see herself in a more detached and objective way.

It goes like this:

1. Do induction and deepening.
2. Set up for "Chair Therapy" where the client can confront or communicate with the Mistake-Making-Part, who will be blamed for every mistake she has ever made in her life.
3. The situation is set up so that the client will be completely safe in expressing her feelings toward the Mistake-Making-Part.
4. The client is encouraged to express how she feels or felt about the mistakes made in her life. The client is greatly encourage to really let it all out.
5. Once the client is exhausted, the therapist has the client take the place of the Mistake-Making-Part, and will speak from that perspective. Before that she was speaking from the perspective of the Self.
6. Therapist then goes after the Mistake-Making-Part, similar to how the client did, but perhaps even stronger.
7. This will often cause new insight in the client with regard to the situation to occur which will be useful in accomplishing the forgiveness of herself.
8. Dialog is encouraged between the client and the Mistake-Making-Part (the client will speak from both perspectives again)

9. The client is then guided into forgiving the Mistake-Making-Part. Because of the new insight, about the situation, the Mistake-Making-Part, can be reframed as the Protective Part, also making her more forgivable.
10. Then additional Direct Suggestion techniques are used, regarding the problem/issue.

This is usually a tremendous experience for the client. By this time in the therapy, the problem has been completely resolved/ healed. The work is usually done at this point and no further work is required. However, sometimes more work may be needed, because of a special circumstance. This will be addressed in Phase V.

Phase V - Parts Mediation Therapy

The vast majority of clients do not need this Phase of the work. It is here for a special case. This is the sticky case of the client that will not heal or completely respond to therapy. This is usually because of Secondary Gain Issues. It must be kept in mind by the enlightened therapist that even some of the most painful problems can have benefits! Phase V, is specifically designed to get at this kind of problem.

It is patterned after two procedures, Parts Therapy and Mediation. Together they become Parts Mediation Therapy. It differs from Parts Therapy because it does not focus on descriptive characteristic of the individual such as the Joy Part, or Creative Part, etc. In that kind of therapy, we are bringing up characteristics or abilities that have been suppressed, lie dormant, or are otherwise out of balance.

In Parts Mediation Therapy, we utilize the concepts of mediation, where we work toward building agreements between the parts of the self which are in conflict. We uncover issues and focus on a win-win situation. These new agreements include doing more beneficial or healthy behaviors in the future.

The process would go like this:

1. Induce hypnosis and deepen.
2. Suggest that you are the mediator and not the judge (mediators are only facilitators).
3. Bring up the subject of the conflict (the problem/issue that has not been completely resolved).
4. Suggest that more communication may be in order.
5. Suggest that there is a part of her that is aware of a benefit of continuing to have the problem.
6. Find out why the problem is useful.
7. Name the part, such as The-Still-Wanting-To-Smoke Part.
8. Have the Self discuss the benefits of making the change.
9. Uncover and discuss alternative behaviors that will provide the same benefits as the problem behavior.
10. Discuss other the benefits of changing to the new behavior.
11. Have both sides come to a win-win agreement where both sides have their needs met.
12. Do any forgiveness work that needs to be done between the two sides.
13. Merge the two sides back together as one.
14. Do Direct Suggestion techniques for change.

As usual, the process ends with appropriate suggestions for change. Here we have uncovered the cause of the inability of the client to come to full resolution of the problem. And, we have provided an alternative, but need fulfilling alternative behavior. This is set up as an agreement between the parts. If there is any reluctance between the parts in this intra-psychic mediation, then a trial period can be agreed upon, where a next session can be set up to evaluate the success of the agreement and make any further changes that may be need to encourage ongoing success.

Summary

This had been a quick overview of 5-PATH a systematic approach to doing hypnotherapy, which is almost universally effective in the problems that our clients face. It can be modified to suit the client and application by the therapist.

I offer training in this system as part of our National Guild of Hypnotists certification course and also as an advanced training for practicing hypnotherapists.

If you have further questions about this process please contact me. www.hypnosiscenter.com

Videos of values

Your behaviour (and that of your clients) is like a video of values. Think about something that you did in the last few days, and imagine that you are watching yourself on a home video. Which of your values were demonstrated? How can you utilise this idea in your client work?

Relax

The time to relax is when you don't have time for it.
Just something that you might like to share with stressed clients!

Security

"Only the insecure strive for security"

Wayne Dyer

Personally I (Fiona) don't subscribe to this view! Doesn't everyone need security? Wayne may be saying that if you have it you don't need to strive for it, but that is tautological. What do you think?

More on security

We have, among other comments, received the following:

I much prefer Tony Robbins quote when he said at one of his seminars "if you want security go to jail!" from Roger Foxwell

And from Jane Watson

What it may refer to is the tendency for the anxiety-prone to prefer avoidance and safety behaviours (security?) to putting themselves in challenging situations. Anyone who works with anxiety disorders will know that an obsession with safety means the client is usually afraid of change (even for-the-better change) because anything that disturbs the routine may have unpredictable consequences. In this way, agoraphobics can settle for isolation, depression, ill health and an empty life, rather than risk a panic attack in the street. Research even finds that our bodies benefit from being challenged (fight infection more efficiently for instance) and that routines and habits - staying within a circumscribed comfort zone - can lead to physical and mental stagnation.

Good points, both. Thank you!

Collusion

I had an interesting client who is having an affair and cannot find a way to reconcile her value systems in that she wants to keep seeing the guy but "knows it is wrong". She constantly seeks other people, including me to tell her what she should do. It is the sort of case in which it would be easy to use my own value system to collude with her, and it is a constant struggle not to. However, I just remember that my role is to help her to decide what is right for her and that my opinions are meaningless. That then makes it easy to avoid colluding!

Using metaphors

The major purpose of a metaphor is to pace and lead a client's behaviour through a story. The major points of construction consist of:

The basic steps to generate a metaphor:

1. Identify the client's issues
2. Strategy analysis
3. Note choices and resources required
4. Establish appropriate anchors to fire off in order to assist the client through the story

Mapping strategies:

1. Remove personal references to the client
2. Pace the client's situation through the story, ensuring that the story avoids direct link between the story and problem
3. Have a route that the client can access in order to resource him/herself
4. Finish the story in a way that the conclusion follows a series of steps that help the character in the metaphor reach a successful conclusion to the issue
5. Use nonsequiturs, ambiguities and direct quotes
6. Keep your resolution as ambiguous as necessary

Looking afresh

To look at something as though we had never seen it before requires great courage.

Henri Matisse

And this is what we are asking clients to do ALL the time!

Window to the world

Better keep yourself clean and bright; you are the window through which you must see the world.

George Bernard Shaw

Discontent

Restlessness and discontent are the first necessities of progress

Edison

Our clients have felt sufficient restlessness and discontent to come to see us: this is a good thing! It's the start of change and we can help them see this as positive.

Questions

No man really becomes a fool until he stops asking questions.

Charles Steinmetz

Therapist's role

Devin Hastings says that the role of a therapist is to help the client to remove blocks to living, and to apply new energy to moving forward. When I heard him say this it struck me as so true that I wanted to share it with you.

Controlling attention

To control attention means to control experience, and therefore the quality of life.

Mihaly Csikszentmihalyi

This guy is the author of wonderful books called "Flow" and "Creativity" among others.

Visualise

To visualise means to make "visual-lies". But then, you (or your client) can make them real!

Integration by separation

This week a client asked me (Fiona) to help her to integrate different elements of her life, and as I was doing the induction I realised that it seemed that there were so many strands that she had identified that I got the image of a bowl of spaghetti and that to work on integration would be creating a splodge of pasta. So instead we worked to separate the strands, almost as if recreating the pack of dried spaghetti before it was cooked. By the way the client liked this analogy!

Freedom

Freedom is what you do with what's been done to you
Jean-Paul Sartre

(submitted by Gloria May)

The power of the mind

I cdnuolt blveiee taht I cluod aulaclty uesdnatnrd what I was rdgnieg. Aoccdrnig to a rscheearch at Cmabrigde Uinervtisy, it deosn't mttaer in what oreddr the ltteers in a word are,
The only iprmoatnt thing is that the frist and lsat ltteer be in the rghit pclae. The rset can be a taotl mses and you can still raed it wouthit a porbelm. This is bcuseae the human mind deos not raed ervey lteter by istlef, but the word as a wlohe.

Amzanig huh?

Perfectionism

Perfection is the dream: the fight to get there is the reality.
Ferrari mechanic's motto

Often clients will have a perfectionist streak that may be interfering with their chances of successfully resolving their issues. If you can help them to see that perfection *IS* something to be aimed for, while always recognising the impossibility of achieving it, you can help them move forward.

Being you

If I won't be myself, who will?

Alfred Hitchcock

I use this quote regularly with clients, and it often touches a cord in somehow a different way from simply saying "be yourself"!

Is life serious?

Not a shred of evidence exists in favor of the idea that life is serious.

Brendan Gill

Maybe this is a little flippant, but many of us often take life and our problems too seriously. But then who is to say what is too seriously, or not seriously enough? This is a personal choice but one which clients (and we?) often forget that we can make. It often takes catastrophic events to put "little" problems into perspective and perhaps an aim of therapy can be to do this on a more regular basis.

Medical pessimism

Things are definitely changing in the medical profession, but there still remains a tendency for some to err on the side of pessimism when dealing with patients. Take the example of a patient who is told that they have cancer and that they would be expected to have only 6 months to live. Of course, that patient is in a suggestible state when they are told this. They are being told by a person in authority and so the "suggestion" takes on extra weight.

I'm not saying that doctors should be unrealistic, or worse, lie to patients, but there are ways to give the truth without giving also the suggestion of failure. In our role as therapists (and human beings) we sometimes have an opportunity to work with this pessimism and turn it around to hope and optimism.

A caveat: if working with serious illness and you are not medically qualified, always work in conjunction with the medical practitioners (pessimistic or not!) to ensure that the client has the best possible care.

Go forwards

Some clients, and therapists, have a tendency to look backwards a lot! But remember, you don't drive a car facing backwards, but you do have a rear view mirror. In order to move forward you need to face front, look where you are going, with occasional glances behind you.

Using adversity

Do you remember how the England players reacted when Rooney was sent off during the 2006 World Cup? They played better than they had all tournament. It was not enough, but they didn't lose to the 11 men of Portugal in the remaining 58 minutes of real play. Isn't this an important factor for clients who are in adversity? It can, but not always, be possible to utilise the bad times to make things better. At the very least the feeling of having done the best one can is helpful.

Erickson's Early Learning Set

Modern hypnotherapy is quite different from the popular conception of hypnosis as a mysterious drama. Therapists are not showmen. They are, however, highly skilled in observation and can recognise even minute variations in behaviour that provide important clues to the client's interests and abilities. These clues are then utilised to help guide the client into altered states of awareness known as trance. Therapy then proceeds by taking the learnings that the person already has an applying them in other ways. Milton Erickson, M.D. was wary about suggesting or adding anything new to the client: he would rather facilitate the client's ability to creatively utilise and develop what he/she already has. The following is Erickson's Early Learning Set Induction.

Get Client to Close His/Her Eyes Then:

When you first went to nursery school, this matter of learning letters and numbers seemed to be a big insurmountable task. To recognise the letter A, to tell a Q from an O was very, very difficult. And then too, joined up writing and print were so different. But you learned to form a mental image of some kind. You didn't know it at the time, but it was a permanent mental image.

And later on in primary school, you formed other mental images of words or pictures of sentences. You developed more and more mental images without knowing you were developing mental images. And you can recall all those images.

Now you can go anywhere you wish, and transport yourself to any situation. You can feel water, you may swim in it, you can do anything you want.

You do not even have to listen to my voice, because your unconscious will hear it. Your unconscious can try anything it wishes. But your unconscious mind isn't going to do anything of importance.

You will notice that your conscious mind is somewhat concerned since it keeps fluttering your eyelids. You have altered your breathing rate, you have altered your pulse, you have altered your blood pressure, and without knowing it, you're demonstrating the immobility that a hypnotic subject can show.

There is nothing really important except the activity of your unconscious mind, and that can be whatever your unconscious mind desires.

Now physical comfort exists, but you do not even need to pay attention to your relaxation and comfort. I can tell your unconscious mind that you are an excellent hypnotic subject, and whenever you need to or want to, your unconscious mind will allow you to use it.

And it can take time, its own time letting you go into trance helping you to understand anything reasonable. When I speak to you it is necessary for you to listen.

I want you to concentrate on all of the wonderful things that makes you unique, that makes you the very special unique person that you are know. And you might take this opportunity to focus on how you can improve on the things in your life that you would like to improve.

(Pause for 5 minutes)

Revive: Notice the body reorientation when you open your eyes and return to full consciousness. Notice how marvellous you feel, and perhaps you might even feel a bit more enlightened about yourself and how you behave.

An interesting question

Kevin Ward from Nottingham emailed us with this interesting idea. He offers a quote: *"the higher the fewer"*. Kevin suggests you then ask people what they think it means.

No two people come up with the same answer. What is interesting is that people in a negative mind set reveal themselves with their answer. Try it with your clients!

Happiness

The U.S. Constitution doesn't guarantee happiness, only the pursuit of it. You have to catch up with it yourself.

Benjamin Franklin

Interesting ideas when working with clients who expect life to be a bowl of cherries!

Negative emotions

What are negative emotions? Anger, fear, sadness? Not necessarily! To me, any emotion is negative if it is inappropriate and any is positive if it is appropriate.

Let's take some examples:

It is appropriate to feel anger if someone has deliberately hurt you and it would be inappropriate in that circumstance to feel joyful!

It is appropriate to feel shame if you have done something that contradicts your value system and if you had it would be inappropriate to feel proud.

It can be really helpful to help your clients recognise this. By doing so, appropriate emotion can be accepted (and if it is uncomfortable, it can be let go of more quickly), and inappropriate emotion can be recognised and dealt with.

Printed in the United Kingdom
by Lightning Source UK Ltd.
136093UK00001B/142-168/P